10 Week Game Plan

for a
Top 100k Blog

by

Kiesha R. Easley

Weblogbetter

10 Week
GAMEPLAN

for a

Top 100k Blog

Kiesha R. Easley

Contents

Bryan – <u>Host with Support</u>

Brian – <u>Blog Engage</u>

Devesh – <u>Blokube</u>

Ana Hoffman <u>Internet Marketing Tools</u>

Andy Bailey – <u>CommentLuv</u>

Marcko – <u>The Traffic Blogger</u>

- Mike Jackness – Best Online Storage
- Aidy – <u>Writing</u>
- David Leonhardt – <u>Blog Writer</u>
- FansBridge.com – <u>How to Market on Facebook</u>
- Sonny – <u>Best WordPress Themes</u>
- Jacob Share – <u>Group Writing Projects</u>
- John Border – <u>Learn how to invest</u>
- Customer Paradigm – <u>Magento Developer</u>
- Wilderness Aware Rafting – <u>Colorado White Water Rafting</u>

A giant *thanks!* goes out to the generous *Surviving the Blog* Contest Sponsors!

copyblogger

Brian Clark CopyBlogger.com

FamousBloggers.net

Twitter

Marketing by
JohnPaulAguiar.com

WordPress   SEO

Ileane – Blogging Tips

Hector Cuevas Blog Marketing Tips

Thesis   Skins by
ThesisAwesome.com

Jane
Sheeba – Successful Blogging

10 Week Game Plan

for a
Top 100k Blog

Intro

When the idea popped into my head to host a reality blogging contest called "Surviving the Blog," I knew I was on to something – but I didn't know that the challenges that I'd devised would have such an impact on the contestant blogs.

As I watched the contest unfold, I learned a great deal from the two teams of bloggers. What happened during the contest makes for such a great case study that I've decided to share it with you in this book. The challenges that the contestants completed have proven to be an effective way to build a successful blog.

At the end of the 10 week contest, the winning blog had a Google Page Rank of 2 and an Alexa ranking of 96,121. If that team could do that in a short 10 weeks, then anyone who is willing to put forth the same strategies could also build a top 100K blog in the same amount of time or less.

In this book, I will highlight the strategies that I believe were the keys that built the winning blog so rapidly. I will also discuss strategies that I use to save time and have worked well for my blog. I'll take you week by week through the challenges and strategies that the teams followed. Of course, I encourage you to go at your own pace if something just isn't feasible for that week. However, if your goal is to build your blog in 10 weeks, it really is important to complete the steps during the week that they are introduced since many of the strategies are extended during next or subsequent weeks.

Even though the contest didn't touch on ways to make money with a blog – I've included a bonus challenge during week 10 that will help you find ways to monetize your growing blog.

Who should read this book and how to use it?

This book will be most helpful for people who are just starting a new blog or who have been struggling with building an audience for an existing blog. It will also be helpful for bloggers who have hit a plateau and just don't know what to do to move beyond that point.

Feel free to skip around or revise challenges that don't apply to you or your niche. If you already have a team, skip the team building section and go straight to the challenges. Feel free to combine challenges and do more than what's prescribed for a particular week. If you want to turn this into a five week game plan by completing two weeks at a time, feel free to do so!

I'm always open to constructive feedback, so let me know what worked well or not so well for you. Feel free to contact me to let me know how you tweaked the plan to meet your needs or if you just want to boast about your success. Your story could get featured on WeBlogBetter.com!

Send your emails to: **kiesha@WeBlogBetter.com**

Affiliate Disclosure

Some, but not all, of the links in this book are affiliate links. This means when you click on links to various sites and/or make a purchase, this could result in me earning a commission on the referred sale.

Some affiliate programs and affiliations include, but are not limited to, ShareaSale, Linkshare, and more. These companies are not affiliated with weblogbetter.com.

If you have questions about any affiliations in this book, please don't hesitate to contact me. I'll be more than happy to clarify or provide additional details if necessary.

3 Winning Strategies

There really is a simple recipe to building the foundation that will support a successful blog. Everything can be summed up to fit within the three following winning strategies.

1. The bloggers blogged as a team.
2. They organized their efforts and divided necessary tasks to complete the weekly challenge.
3. They took action and did their best to adhere to deadlines.

In this section, we'll take a closer look at each of these strategies and how you can apply them to your blogging efforts.

Winning Strategy #1: Work as a Team

I've said this before: team blogging makes a world of difference when you're trying to start a new blog. Finding the right bloggers to team up with is the key to getting a new blog out of that lonesome no traffic state that plagues so many new blogs.

It really has to be a good mix of organized go-getters, though – as I saw in this contest, the team that couldn't get itself organized and rowing in the same direction, was the team that failed.

Why does team blogging work so well? Because it allows you create more content at a more frequent and steady pace than you could alone. It also gives you more outlets and opportunities for promotion. It extends your blog's reach.

How to Build a Successful Team

There is no way on earth that I would've been able to continue building WeBlogBetter.com if I hadn't found a group of enthusiastic bloggers to team up with. For the first six or seven months that I owned the blog, I produced pretty much all of the contest myself with the exception of a guest blogger or two.

Every day, I worked diligently to publish fresh content, come rain or shine. Of course, there were days that I was exhausted, but I was determined to pull it off. The blog was growing and everything was going well, but then I hit a snag.

That year, my family relocated to a new state. It was a big move and I knew I was going to be without a reliable internet connection for at least a few weeks. There was no way I'd be able to keep writing and publishing every day on my own.

So a few weeks before the move, I contacted several of my blogging friends and proposed that they write regularly for the site. They each took a different day of the week to publish fresh content. They were free to add links to their sites as well as affiliate links. They each had blogs of their own and could benefit from the traffic that I'd built, so it was a win/win situation.

I was able to keep in contact with everyone via email on my cell phone and even though I was without internet longer than I had anticipated, I was able to keep my blog going because I had scheduled content ahead of time and was able to maintain it with a few trips to the library.

That was a pivotal moment for me, because I was at a point where I really could've let my blog die, but I just couldn't stand the thought of letting all of my previous hard work go to waste. It was also a significant moment because it showed me how much you can accomplish when you work as a team.

We each worked to promote each other's blogs and I also contributed content to their blogs whenever I could.

I found that when I worked with a team, it reduced my stress level and extended my blog's audience. What would have normally been one tweet from my Twitter account suddenly became 3-4 additional tweets from each of my team mates' accounts.

It also meant that whenever they published posts on my blog, we both benefitted mutually. They benefitted from having access to my blog's audience and traffic and I benefitted from the content and also the people they brought to the blog.

It was at that point that I realized that blogging alone was just not an efficient or effective way to work.

The group of bloggers that I've worked with has evolved as some of them have come and gone. At times, it got a little frustrating, but I didn't let it get the best of me. I just kept on searching for new people to build mutually beneficial blogging relationships and kept it moving.

Along the way, I've found that there really are some key things to keeping people motivated and keeping things mutually beneficial.

The keys to building a great blogging team:

1. **Identify like-minded bloggers.** Your blogging niches don't have to be exactly the same, but should at least be

related. This makes it easier to cross-promote on each other's blogs and social networking sites.

2. **Establish an agreed upon mode of communication.** Set up a virtual meeting time/place such as chats, hangouts, FB groups. It may be difficult to get everyone together at the same time, especially if you have team members who live in other countries. I found that just having a group where we could all post announcements and then check whenever we got a free moment worked out well.

3. **Help each other.** The best way to strengthen a team is to commit to helping each other as often as possible. Exchange banner ads, display each other's links; promote each other's ebooks, products or services. Share each other's content on social networks – in other words, go out of your way for each other. Celebrate each other's successes – you never know when one of you will make it big, and if one makes it, chances are you'll all make it!

During the Surviving the Blog contest, the team that was able to bring all of these things together was the one that survived.

Even when it got to the point in the contest where the team members were competing against each other, they refused to throw each other to the wolves. They stuck together and helped each other, even if it meant they were jeopardizing their own chance at winning the $1000 Grand Prize.

In the end they were able to remain friends, and to this day, they all still contribute to the winning blog.

Individual vs. Team Blogging (Pros/Cons)

Obviously, there are some pros and cons to both blogging alone and blogging with a team. I'm a firm believer that there are no one-size-fits-all solutions, so I thought it would be a good idea to point out some of the drawbacks and perks of both. That way, you can compare and make a choice that best fits your needs.

The blogging strategies will still work, but of course results will vary and it may take longer to reach your goals.

Let's take a look at some of the pros of blogging individually, without a team.

Pros of Blogging Alone

Complete Control – When you blog alone, it's pretty obvious that you're in complete control of your domain (both literally and figuratively). You decide what you'll write and when.

Dependability – You don't have to depend on anyone but yourself – that means there will be no disappointments when people suddenly get too busy to submit posts. You've already got it covered – or not!

Predictability – When you blog alone, there will be no surprise off-topic posts or posts with too many affiliate or self-promotional links. No worries about having to edit or suddenly write a post on a day when someone else was supposed to submit something. When you set your posting schedule it's set until you want to change it.

Stability – Because you are the sole blogger (with an occasional guest blogger), you get an opportunity to share more of yourself with your audience and thereby creating a more stable stock of loyal readers who want to read what you have to say.

Cons of Blogging Alone

Work Overload – Blogging alone means all of the blogging tasks are yours alone. There's no one to divide tasks among – it's all on you! Even when you have blog maintenance tasks or technical issues to tend to, you're still expected to write and promote your posts. It's easy to get burned out and when that happens. Most people quit just when they're about to get their breakthrough.

Not Enough Time – You'll find yourself always running out of time because there's just not enough time do everything that needs to be done to build and promote your blog. Because of the amount of time it takes to write a post and also promote on social networks, it may mean that you'll have to settle for less frequent updates.

Not Enough Reach – Since it's just you, you'll have less reach when it comes to promoting on social networks. Of course, you can schedule and spread your tweets out during the day, but you'll still only get one tweet at time – when blogging with a team, you get additional shares and will gain greater influence.

What to do if you don't have a team?

Obviously, everyone can't work with a team. For various reasons that range from being a new blogger to simply preferring to work alone. Does this mean that you can't achieve a top 100K ranking in the same amount of time? Of course not!

However, you still must consider the downsides that I've mentioned above. You'll have to work harder and spend more time working on your blog. It can be done if you're driven enough and can focus your energy on the most important tasks and avoid getting distracted.

For whatever reason, if you choose to blog alone, as you encounter the weekly tasks, don't allow yourself to become overwhelmed. First, focus on the absolutely most necessary ongoing blogging tasks before moving on to the other parts of the challenges.

No matter what the challenge of the week is be sure to complete these most essential tasks:

1. **Publish content at predictable intervals.** In other words, create a schedule and stick to it. If you decide that you want to post on Mondays, Wednesdays and Fridays, be consistent and post on those days no matter what.

2. **Share your content on the most popular social networks.** Focus on just 3, no more than 4 popular social networks. Stick with promoting on Twitter, Facebook and Google+ or whichever networks are most popular and appropriate for your niche.

3. **Network and connect with others.** You can't ever know too many people. The more people you connect with, the greater your chances for success. You never know which connection will lead you to that editor at the

publishing house or which connection will give you valuable information about an opportunity you've been looking for. Even if the people you connect with do nothing more than share your content with their friends, it's still worth taking the time to connect.

While you may be set to work alone, I highly recommend eventually building up enough relationships with others so that you can at least have a group of allies to turn to from time to time.

Now, let's take a look at some of the pros of blogging with a team.

Pros of Blogging with a Team

Help with Writing – Even if you only get someone to commit to writing one post per month, that's one extra post that you don't have to write. This can free up some of your time to focus on other tasks.

Help with Promoting – Nothing is better than a team of bloggers who share each other's content faithfully. Of course, you all should be producing quality content that would be valuable to each other's followers – the quickest way to loose trust is to post questionable content on social networks. So, make sure you're working with people who have the same standards of quality as you do.

More Heads, Better Ideas – Creativity and a source of fresh ideas is an amazing asset when it comes to blogging because things can get stale very quickly. When you have more people to brainstorm with and share ideas, you tend to get richer, more innovative ideas that can leave a greater mark.

Larger Audience, Larger Reach – When you work with a great team of bloggers, you get an opportunity to borrow their audience whenever they post on your blog. When they share the link to their post on their own blog and via their social network accounts, their readers will flock to read their content.

If the new visitors like your blog, they may stick around and become loyal readers of your blog, too. These are people you may not have had access to otherwise.

Cons of Blogging with a Team

It Takes Time to Find Good Team Mates – Of course, building a successful team is not always as easy as it sounds. To avoid headaches and major problems that could ruin your blogging efforts, it's imperative that you find trust-worthy, dependable, dedicated to quality, like-minded bloggers.

Unpredictability – Of course you and your team can plan which topics everyone will cover ahead of time, but there's still no way to know exactly what they're going to write until they've written it. You and your team might also decide on a predetermined deadline for submissions, but often you won't know until the last minute when someone is going to miss a post. So, it's a good idea to stay prepared with an extra post on hand in the event of an unexpected missed deadline.

Losing Team Members – The team of bloggers that I've worked with has changed several times. Why? Not because we fell out or got mad at each other, but simply because people's goals change, people get tired of blogging altogether, or simply because people have lives beyond the blogosphere, obviously. No matter what the reason, it still sucked to get that dreaded message from a blogger who would no longer be able to contribute regularly to the blog. But as long as you don't take it personal, you can usually part as friends and continue to help each other in other ways.

What to do if a Team Member Quits?

During the Surviving the Blog Contest, at the end of the week, the team had to vote off a member. This meant the team had less people to work with. That meant less content and less help to complete some of the tasks. It was the most dreaded part of the contest.

Over the course of the last few years, I've had several people decide that working closely as a team to produce content for my blog was not for them any longer. I wasn't paying them beyond sharing my audience and allowing them to post affiliate links, so who was I to get mad at them? We're all human right?

So, instead of dwelling on them leaving, I simply approached other bloggers to see if they were interested in becoming regular contributors. The idea isn't for everyone, but for people who are looking to build their sphere of influence, the opportunity to get their writing in front of an established blog every week without having to keep pitching guest posts to blog owners is a good deal.

So when a blogger you've teamed up with needs to quit or reduce their posting frequency, happily give them their freedom. Express your willingness to remain friends and continue helping each other and then simply look for some new bloggers to partner up with. That's why it's so important to keep networking and connecting, you'll always have people you can team up with.

Who Should You Contact and What Should You Say?

For some people this may be obvious, but I wanted to make sure everyone is fully equipped with the tools to succeed. If you're outgoing, you probably already know what to do and what to say, but if you're a bit shy, then the thought of approaching people with a proposition probably makes you feel a little uncomfortable. (I'm a shy person at heart, so I know how you feel!) But no worries, if you know how to send an email, then you can do this part.

First, make a list of potential bloggers you'd like to contact – at least 15 different people. Make sure these are people that you've already connected with and are familiar with their writing style. This isn't the time to contact random people. They should be in a related blogging niche, but again, I say this loosely because sometimes unusual joint ventures work – think about Starbucks and Barnes & Noble (books and coffee).

While it's probably best to start small and start with people who have approximately the same level of experience as you do, I'd never tell you shy away from anyone. You just never know what could happen – they might say "yes" – the worse they could say is "no" – you have nothing to lose by asking. The goal is to get

3 – 5 people to commit to working with you and to contributing regular content to your blog.

Now when I say regular, it doesn't matter how regular as long as they can be consistent, so let them know that you're okay with a commitment of weekly, every-other-weekly, or even monthly posts. Just keep at it until you have enough people to fill the slots you need.

Next, compose a quick, to the point, but personalized email message. It must be personal – so highlight some things about the person that you've noticed or that you admire. Then tell them about your plans to form a team and why you think they'd make a great team mate. Share with them your goals and the mutual benefits that working together would bring.

Once you've gotten enough positive responses, it's time to assemble. The next section will tell you how to organize your team and strategize your plan of attack for achieving top 100k status.

Winning Strategy #2: Organize your efforts

Identify Strengths and Divide Tasks Accordingly

In order to get the best out of your team, it's better to let each member decide on a topic of focus based on his or her strengths and interests rather than telling them what you want. They'll naturally produce higher quality articles that they'll want to promote more enthusiastically.

If you'd like to get fancy with titles, make them the editor of a particular category of your blog. For example, if you've got a travel blog – one team member could be the "Local Foodie

Editor" while another could be the "Hotel Reviews Editor." These editors would be in charge of whatever research tasks are necessary to compose a weekly (bi-weekly or monthly) post. They would also be responsible for promoting that post and moderating and/or responding to comments.

If you have a team member who's more experienced or comfortable with promoting on social networks, you could assign them to be the "Social Media Manager" if they're interested.

Getting organized this way makes it much easier to manage things more efficiently.

Establish and agree on deadlines up front

To avoid confusion and unnecessary frustration, it's important to establish and agree upon deadlines well in advance. While it would be ideal to get submissions a week or two in advance, it might be more realistic to set the deadline 4-5 days before the post is expected to go live. The more in advance you set the deadline, the more flexibility you'll have to work with if someone can't produce a post for that week.

Planning ahead also makes it easier to create more cohesive content. As a team you can decide on a theme for each week. It's so much easier to write when you've got a central theme to focus on. This will allow you to create series, a strategy that increases page views and encourages people to click from post to post.

Obviously, you'll need to decide on deadlines that work best for you and your team.

Winning Strategy #3: Take Action

Complete tasks as agreed upon

The best plans and intentions mean absolutely nothing if they never get put into action! I'm guilty of this. It's so easy to get caught up in the exciting planning phase. For some reason, it's during that stage that I'm the most motivated. As soon as it's time for me to actually do something, I suddenly don't feel like it. It helps to break the tasks down into pieces - that makes it easier for me to kick things into gear.

Create a to-do list for yourself and your team and schedule a time when you will complete them. Just creating the list isn't enough – you have to actually take a close look at your schedule so that you'll know for sure which times you have available.

I actually set times for when I'll complete tasks. I schedule them in my phone and set an alarm to remind me. I do this because with so many things vying for my attention, it's so easy for me to forget.

Obviously, you can't control what your team members will be doing, but you can send out deadline reminders and make sure you stick to the deadlines you've set for yourself.

Progress Updates

While you don't need to keep up with everyone every single day, it's a good idea to touch bases with each other once or twice a week. It's a good idea to establish a Facebook group or another place where each of you can post updates that everyone can check when they get a moment.

I found that trying to meet up online at a specific time didn't work well since everyone doesn't live in the same time zone, but it's not impossible. Try to organize a live chat with your team and see how it goes. Even if you just get a couple of members together, you can always catch the others up later. It's much easier to collaborate this way when you can get immediate feedback and responses.

The team that can effectively communicate is the team that will achieve the most success, so make it a priority to stay in touch. Keeping everyone updated and being able to communicate with each other will help things run more smoothly.

Also, encourage your team members to post things that they'd like help promoting. Encourage them to post links they'd like tweeted or shared on social networks. This is a good way to keep track of what everyone is doing on their own blogs, and it makes it easier for everyone to chip in and cross promote each other.

TwitterFeed to Automate Cross Promotion

With so many different tasks that need to be done, it's always great when you can automate some things. You can automate part of your team's cross promotion efforts by using Twitterfeed.com

Twitterfeed is a site that automatically tweets out new updates from your favorite blogs. It also allows you to post to Facebook. It's a great site to use so that you won't forget to share your team members' blog updates.

If you don't already have an account set up, it's easy to get started. Start by creating an account, then click "Create a Feed" and follow all of the steps to add each one of your team members' feeds. For each feed, go to the "Advanced Settings" link to adjust your settings and personalize the tweet by adding your team mates' Twitter IDs.

After you've adjusted your settings, click "Continue to Step 2", you'll need to authorize your Twitter and Facebook accounts to complete the process for each blog.

Encourage each member complete this process to include everyone's blogs. Don't forget to add your own blog's feed to your Twitterfeed account.

Each week, you'll read about the challenges the Surviving the Blog teams completed and how you can apply those strategies to your blog.

The challenges are organized in a logical progression for building a blog. They build on each other and some will be ongoing activities that you should continue doing even after that particular week is over. All of the challenges are promotional in nature and are geared to improve one or more aspects of your blog as well as bring in more traffic.

From a management perspective, it's probably easier to ask each team member to focus on the blog posts that they contribute rather than trying to help promote the entire blog. They should complete the tasks associated with that week's challenge to promote their blog post.

If you have the budget for it, and you want to make things interesting for your team, you could treat it like a contest and offer incentives for the members who promote their posts the best. $25-$50 Gift cards or PayPal funds make great incentives.

How to Proceed Through the Challenges

For those who haven't already started their blogs, I've included every challenge from the Surviving the Blog contest here – including the first one that the two teams completed. That challenge gives a quick glimpse of things to consider when you're just starting out.

However, I realize there are others who already have their blog started and may have already done some of the things mentioned in a particular challenge. If this is the case, feel free to skip whichever tasks that you feel are unnecessary.

Of course, I encourage you to read each challenge carefully before you make a decision about its necessity. You may discover a different way to do something or may find ways to automate tasks. Finding a way to save time is always on my mind, so I'll be sharing information about tools that help me use my time more efficiently.

So let's move on to the challenges and discuss the strategies that will help you on your way to becoming a top 100k blog over the next ten weeks.

Week 1 Challenge: Starting a Blog

There are so many small pieces involved in starting a blog. I remember being so utterly confused in those beginning days. What took me years to learn about the essentials for building a solid foundation for a blog is all right here – an instant shortcut for those who just don't know what to do or where to start.

So, it's pretty natural and obvious that the first challenge for the Surviving the Blog contest would have the teams Setup and Design their blogs!

The team members had to work together to come up with and agree on a suitable domain name and then quickly created an eye-catching design. They also had to scramble to get social networking accounts setup and even get their very first blog post published! They had to do that all before the end of the first week.

So here are your tasks for this week:

- Decide on a Domain Name to register and self-host.
- Install WordPress and decide on a template to customize or design from scratch.
- Install Plugins (see p. 28 for a list of suggested plugins).
- Create Basic Pages.
- Set up Social Media Accounts.
- Set up a Feedburner Account to Manage RSS.

Decide on a domain name to register and self-host

You may want to call on your team for help with selecting a domain name or you may work on this on your own. You may already have a name in mind, but it might be a good idea to bounce ideas around with your team – you never know, you may come up with something better.

You'll want to a select a name that's pretty well connected to your niche. As much as you may like a name, this is not the time to be clever - this is a time to be clear. So if you plan to blog about gardening, then you need the word "garden" or "gardening" somewhere in your domain name.

Example: GreatGardeningTips.com

This helps search engines when determining what your site is about, so make it easy for them – select a name that coincides with your niche. You can always add a fun tagline that helps you define your site even more.

A domain name shouldn't be long and drawn out, it should be as short as possible – probably no more than 4 words. It should be easy to remember. A dot-com (.com) extension is preferable, but if your name is already taken, you might want to consider a dot-net (.net) or even dot-org (.org). If all of those are taken, you may need to add another word or be more specific.

Example: SherrysGardeningTips.com

For more tips on selecting an appropriate domain name, check out these blog posts:

- "Naming the blog"
  http://weblogbetter.com/2012/02/10/naming-the-blog/
- "A Killer Domain Name: The Most Important Blog Decision"
  http://weblogbetter.com/2010/12/13/a-killer-domain-name-the-most-important-blogging-decision/

Hosting & Domain Registry Pricing

If you're not already aware of pricing, domain names can range from $1 - $15 depending on where you register them. Some webhosts offer free domain registration with the purchase of a year of hosting. As of July 2012, Justhost.com is offering free registration when you use their shared hosting platform which ranges in price, starting at about $60-75 a year.

If you've already selected a different host, then I've found Netfirms.com to be the cheapest place to register a domain name. You don't have to host your domain on their site, you can host it anywhere. Just register with them and then point your name servers to wherever you're going to host your blog's files. Currently (July 2012), they've got first time registration for as low as $6.95 a year, but even their renewal rate is still only $11.99 a year after that – still cheaper than $15.

Install WordPress and decide on a template

Collaborate on creating a design from scratch or work together to find a template that you all agree on.

The quickest way to get started is to select a pre-made template and then personalize it with your own header, layout and color tweaks.

If you've got the knowledge and skills, arranging your own code is the best way to ensure you've got an original design. I prefer to tweak pre-designed templates. It's quicker and easier to get up and running in a day or two this way. I recommend using the Genesis Framework. They've got lots of great child-themes that are easier to tweak and you can change up the layout by moving around your widgets or making slight code customizations.

The Surviving the Blog winners at TheNextGoal.com, started by choosing the Tapestry Theme – they added a customized header, tweaked the color and a few other features to create an original look.

Those simple changes made all the difference and helped them create an inviting design in a very short time. This blog went from the idea stage to up and running in less than a week. I don't think that would've been possible if they'd chosen to design from scratch.

Install Plugins

Plugins add functionality and interactivity to a blog easily without coding. Obviously, if you know how to code, you probably won't need as many. I've listed a few suggested plugins below, but select only the ones that you'll need and use since plugins tend to slow down a blog's loading time. Your needs will vary depending on your niche.

You can find these plugins by logging into your WordPress admin panel. Go to "Plugins" > "Add New" – conduct a search using the names listed below. I've added the name of the creator to the plugins that have more than one with the same name.

List of Suggested Plugins:

- All in One Favicon (be sure to add a favicon)
- BackupWordpress
- CommentLuv
- Contact Form 7
- Do Follow (by Denis de Bernardy)
- Easy Twitter Button (by DolcePixel)
- Facebook Like Box (add to sidebar widget)
- FD FeedBurner Plugin (redirect feeds to feedburner)
- GetSocial

- Google Analyticator (Use same account for Google+, Feedburner)
- Headspace2
- JetPack (I recommend for Stats only, but there are other options available)
- LinkWithin (must get from linkwithin.com) or other related posts plugin
- MaxBlogPress Ping Optimizer (get this one from Maxblogpress site:
  http://www.maxblogpress.com/plugins/mpo/ (free plugins) – scroll down, click to download, then add a list of sites you'd like to ping. See below for a list of suggested sites to ping)
- No self pings
- Print Friendly and PDF (optional)
- ReplyMe
- RSS Footer (optional)
- Scribe
- W3 Total Cache
- WP-BlogEngage (get from Blog Engage site – buttons)
- WP-Optimize
- WPBook – auto post to Facebook FanPage Wall

What is Pinging and Why is it Important?

Whenever you write a new blog post, pinging will let various search engines and other sites know that there's something new on your site. This helps your site potentially get search engine traffic quicker than it normally would.

If you went to the site to download the free plugin from Maxblogpress, you would've found more information about this there and why it's a good idea to use their plugin instead of letting WordPress do it for you.

If you didn't take the time to read it, now's a good time to go back and give it a closer read and learn more about how pinging effects your blog:

- "Using WordPress Can Ban Your Blog From Ping Services"
  http://www.maxblogpress.com/plugins/mpo/

Suggested Sites to Ping

Copy and paste the following list into your MaxBlogPress Ping Optimizer settings if you chose to download the plugin. If you don't want the plugin, use Sherryl Perry's instructions at this link:
"How to Ping Your Blog and When Not To"
http://keepupwiththeweb.com/how-to-ping-your-website-blog-and-when-not-to/.

http://pingomatic.com/
http://pingler.com/
http://www.pingmyblog.com/
http://autopinger.com/
http://www.ping.in/
http://www.kping.com/
http://feedping.com/
http://feedping.com/
http://pingoat.net/
http://totalping.com/
http://www.pingates.com/
http://www.feedshark.brainbliss.com/
http://feedburner.google.com/fb/a/ping

http://blo.gs/
http://blogbuzzer.com
http://www.pingmylink.com
(I found this list at: "Top 15 Blog Ping Services"
http://keepupwiththeweb.com/how-to-ping-your-website-blog-and-when-not-to/)

Create Basic Pages

In addition to the obvious home page, every blog should have at least the following basic pages:

- **About** – this page should welcome readers to your blog and should tell them what types of posts they can expect to read while visiting your blog. This is a great opportunity to invite them to subscribe and to check out some of your most popular posts. So be sure to go back and update this page periodically – at least once a year.

- **Contact** – this page should give your readers a way to contact you either by email or by completing a form (Contact 7 plugin creates forms for you). You can add as much or as little contact information as you'd like. It's also a good idea to let them know how quickly you intend to respond – 24-48 hours is a widely accepted timeframe.

- **Privacy Policy** – Google likes sites to inform readers about how their personal information will be used. You can get a free Privacy Policy to copy and paste right into your blog by going to FreePrivacyPolicy.com.

- **Affiliate Disclosure** – this page is only necessary if you intend to monetize your site. If you're planning on displaying advertisements or affiliate links, you need to create this page to maintain transparency. Most affiliate programs require you do this anyway, so you might as well create it from the beginning. If don't want to create a separate page for this, an alternative is to place a short statement in the footer of your blog and also on your About page. You can find an example of an appropriate statement here:
The FTC, Affiliate Disclosure & You:
http://blog.2createawebsite.com/2009/12/07/the-ftc-affiliate-disclosure-and-you/.

Failure to add this statement could result in your various affiliate accounts being suspended, your blog being reported or worse.

Social Media Account Setup:

You may already have accounts set up at various social networking sites, however, with the exception of Facebook, it might a good idea to create new accounts using your domain name as username and creating a new profile to reflect your new site wherever possible. This doesn't mean you have to close your other accounts – you can still use them – but creating accounts that are clearly connected to your blog will strengthen your brand and will help you create a more influential presence on the web.

There are new sites popping up every day – I'd be crazy if I tried to list them all, so I've listed a few that I use below. You decide if you want to join these or additional sites that you're interested in.

- Twitter
- FaceBook Fanpage
- Google+
- LinkedIn
- Blog Engage
- Blog Interact
- Blokube
- BizSugar
- Pinterest

Be sure to add a photo of yourself or a logo that you've created for your blog and a short bio to your profile page. Include links to your new blog and let people know what types of posts or updates they can expect to see.

Spend some time following new people every day. Don't worry if they don't follow back, if you're interested in what they're posting, that's good enough.

After you've created your new social networking accounts, to work more efficiently, it's a good idea to manage some of them with Hootsuite.

Tools to Manage and Schedule Tweets

I absolutely love it when a tool saves me and trouble! Hootsuite.com is a social media dashboard that allows you to access various social networking sites at once – it makes it easier to view and manage your social media profiles. So far, Hootsuite works with Twitter, Facebook and LinkedIn.

I like it because it allows me to manage my Twitter accounts and let me see my feed, mentions, direct messages, scheduled messages and my tweeted messages all on one page. This makes it easier for me to keep up and respond to messages that are just for me.

My favorite Hootsuite feature, hands down, is the ability to schedule messages for a later time. This is important for several reasons. It lets me spread out my tweets so that my followers are not blasted by too many messages at once and it lets me post things at a prime time even when I'm not available. It gives me an opportunity to get exposure even in the middle of the night while I'm sleeping – this means that my followers who are in an entirely different time zone can still see my tweets! I can use it with more than one Twitter account for even greater efficiency!

It can also be used in the same way with Facebook and LinkedIn– so it means you only have to go to one site to manage all three of these popular social networks. You can post one message to all of your streams at once allowing you to efficiently and effectively connect with your audiences at these different sites without having to keep logging in or clicking from site to site.

Setup a Feedburner Account to Manage RSS

When you set up a WordPress blog, it generally creates your feed automatically. Your feed allows people to subscribe to your blog and receive updates via email or an RSS reader. This lets them view your updates without physically visiting your blog.

Your feed link is usually your www.domainname.com/feeds/ or something similar. That's great and it will work fine, but if you want to be able to monetize your feed later on with Google Adsense, then you'll need to set up your feeds at Feedburner.

Feedburner.com is free. It enables your Adsense code to be displayed in your feeds. When a subscriber reads an item from your feed (via email or in a reader), if they click an ad, or if your feed gets a certain number of views, you'll be compensated just as you would if they were on your site. It pays slightly less per click, but it's still worth setting up.

You'll be able to connect to Feedburner using your Google (or Gmail) account if you have one, otherwise you can start from scratch and set it up. Once your account set up is completed, you'll be able to add your blog's feed and adjust your settings by clicking on the various tabs which include "Monetize".

While you're there, be sure to enable the email subscriptions feature under the "Publicize" tab – click "Email Subscriptions" and then scroll down to make the service "Active." You may notice that there are subscription forms available there, but I recommend using the forms from an email service such as Mailchimp.com – we'll talk more about this free service in the upcoming weeks.

This concludes this week's challenge. These tasks make up the basic foundation that will help you promote your blog. Now that you know what you need to do, contact your team and set these tasks into motion.

Week 1 Challenge Recap: Starting a Blog

- Decide on a domain name to register.
- Install WordPress and decide on design.
- Install Plugins & create Basic Pages.
- Set up Social Media Accounts.
- Set up a Feedburner Account.

Week 2 Challenge: Quality Content Generation

The more content a new blog has, the more likely it will capture the attention of the search engines and most importantly, loyal readers.

It doesn't matter if you can generate a boat load of traffic to a site if there's no reason for people to hang around. You want people to be able to dive into your site, to be able to click around and just soak up all of the awesome knowledge that you have to share.

So this leads me to this week's challenge -

Quality Content Generation

During the Surviving the Blog contest, the contestants were challenged with the task of producing at least two posts per day during that week. For most bloggers, that schedule is insane and not sustainable. So, my recommendation for you is this: if you and your team can produce two posts or more per day, then go for it. The more content you can produce, the quicker you'll establish your blog.

If not, focus on producing one post for every weekday and make that your goal. These posts should be no less than about 400 words – longer posts tend to rank better. Your posts should be original content – no spun content or duplicated content from article directories.

These posts should be foundational in nature – in other words, they should set the tone for the types of posts your blog will continue to produce. They should help you define your categories. I recommend writing at least one post for each category during this week.

How many categories should a blog have?

It all depends on your blog's niche. Obviously, the more general your blog, the more potential categories you'll have. But here's my loose rule of thumb: 5, but no more than 10. Or if you want to keep it visually simple, don't add more categories than will fit one line on your blog's main navigation menu. Menus than run over to two lines tend to look messy and unorganized. So challenge yourself to keep your topics within what'll fit on your menu.

Optimize your posts

I can't lie and say that SEO is the most enjoyable part of blogging, however, it is necessary. Organic search traffic is free – that means no ads are required to get people to your site if you produce valuable content that people are looking for – every blog post you create is a potential free ad that could bring countless people to your site.

I hated the idea of it in the beginning, but once I finally stopped fighting it, I realized the small steps I took to optimize my content made a huge difference – every day that I published something new brought more and more people. After that point, I realized a smart blogger knows that you need to optimize your content if you expect it to be seen by more than your friends and family.

In a blog post Tia Peterson (BizChickBlogs.com) wrote for WeBlogBetter, she discusses some of the easiest ways to optimize individual blog posts for search engines. I still find this post to be one of the most simplified ways to approach SEO.

It addresses what you can do to optimize your individual posts and focuses on the most basic aspects of optimization that can increase your chances of receiving free search engine traffic. So as you write your posts, be sure to add the elements Tia mentions below.

Complete Guide to Easy SEO for Busy Bloggers

The life of a busy blogger is all play and no fun. Wait – is that right? More like all blogging and no SEO! Optimizing each post for proper search engine indexing and better search engine ranking can be annoying and time consuming. Some bloggers have written it off altogether.

Woah, there!

Don't write off blog SEO. You will regret it if you do. We talk this subject to death and people get sick off of it and turn away, but it's worth paying attention to these tips because they are easy and will go an extra-long way toward increasing your individual post page rank, search engine ranking for your blog in general, and will increase traffic over time.

Think Top Down
The most important elements on your page in terms of SEO are the page title, the URL, and the h1 tag. If you have a WordPress blog, you're in luck because you can control all three of these elements easily.

The Scary, Ugly Truth

All of this is subject to change. To me, that's the most important reason NOT to check out of SEO class too early. At least stay tuned, because as search engines get smarter and make better indexing decisions, things change and what was once important becomes less important.

#1: Page Title

The page title is NOT the post title; don't get confused about that.

Here is what the page title looks like in a browser:

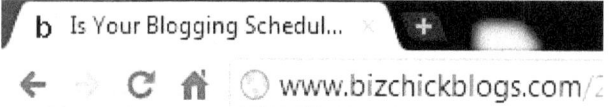

It's the text that appears at the very top of your browser window. Depending on your blog's site configuration, this is usually the same as the post title.

Sometimes, the blog's name precedes the post title, and that is a big no-no. This can easily be fixed in WordPress if you use All in One SEO or have Thesis theme for WordPress, but it can also be fixed on Blogger blogs. In terms of on-page SEO, this is the top and most important element to get right.

#2: URL – Shorten that slug!

Again, this is an area WordPress users can easily manage that Blogger users cannot. Search engines, particularly Google, pay very close attention to URLs when trying to determine how relevant a page is to a keyword.

Your slug is the portion of the URL that applies to your post specifically (see below). Your keywords should be at the very beginning of that slug.

Tip: For best practices, simply reduce the slug to just the keyword itself. Not only does this make for a better, shorter URL all around, it's very clear what the post is about.

#3 The h1 tag – the Post Title (usually)

WordPress default functionality makes the page and post titles the h1 tag on single post pages. The h1 tag tells search engines, "this is the name of this page." It's a header. Like a section header in a book. You only need 1 of these! Only the first one counts. So if you're using WordPress, don't apply the h1 tag to other text in the post.

Why the h1 tag: Back in the day, search engine algorithms placed significant importance on two major things: the very first text to show up on a page, and the largest text to show up on a page. With the implementation of the h1 tag, people no longer need to specially format their text so it's much larger than all of the other text. It's still pretty important to put the h1 tag first, but it's not as crucial now.

For WordPress blogs, the h1 tag on your home page will differ based on your theme. Thesis themes use the tagline as the h1, which is very smart. All you have to do is make your tagline keyword-rich and you're good to go. Other themes may simply use all of the post titles on the home page as h1 which is less effective, as only one h1 will count.

Tip: Your post title needs to contain keywords, but it also needs to be written for human readers! A smart trick is to use colons or dashes to separate the keyword out, and then add a nicely written title after it. For example, "Cheap Sesame Street Videos: Great Places to Find Them" as opposed to "Great Places to Find Cheap Sesame Street Videos." This is especially important with very competitive phrases.

#4 Inbound Links Anchored with Keywords

This is simple: pick up some keyword-contextual inbound links.

Easy ways to do it:

When blogging on open platforms such as BlogHer (or other social networking sites), create a signature that contains anchor text links.

Vary your author resource boxes in article directories so it links to a specific post.

Use a service like Amplify to create a single sentence blog update that links anchor text to your new post.

Tia Peterson is founder and principal of Webbed Ink, Inc. , a web content strategy consultancy based in Tucson, Arizona. She created BizChickBlogs - a blog offering practical, usable advice for bloggers.

Simple as that! Those are just a few ideas. Do that a lot, and do it differently based on specific posts.

Special Tip for Amplify: If you write a post on Pilates exercise videos, update your Amplog (your Amplify blog) with a sentence like, "Just published a post on Pilates exercise videos that lists four places to find them for under $10. Have a look!" Link 'Pilates exercise videos' to your new post, and when you update your Amplog, be sure to connect all of the services to it

(Blogger, Tumblr, Diigo, Plurk, etc.) so that your anchor text link gets everywhere.

Don't go overboard! Quite frankly, for many of your posts, if the target keyword is largely non-competitive, one to two inbound anchor text links is going to be enough, and then if your content is sticky, more people will link to it on your behalf so you don't need to. Contrary to popular belief, most people publishing content on the Internet know little to nothing about SEO. You are at a major advantage.

SEO-Related Posts You Might Want to Read

Take the time now to educate yourself on just a little bit of on-page SEO. Here are some posts you should bookmark and read when you've got time:

- "5 SEO tips for bloggers that won't make people gouge their eyes out" http://weblogbetter.com/2010/05/22/blogging-tips-seo-for-blogger/
- "Top 10 Free SEO Tips for Beginners (Post Panda and Penguin)" http://www.minterest.com/top-10-free-seo-tips-for-beginners/

More Tips to Maximize Your SEO Efforts

Tia's post quickly covered some essentials, but I'd add a few more steps to make it easier for your posts to turn up in search engines.

Use Headspace2 Plugin and Add a Description

I mentioned the Headspace plugin in last week's challenge, but if you decided not to install the plugin, here's why you should go back and add it. Headspace adds additional fields to your

Wordpress Post Editor that allow you to add a Page Title (as Tia mentioned) and also a description.

HeadSpace

Page Title: Strategies for Increasing Subscribers to your Blog

Description: Competition for the attention of blog readers is high; bloggers are continually looking for new ways to increase their number of subscribers.

9 remaining

advanced

This description is important because sometimes search engines include them in search results. It makes your individual blog posts more discoverable. So it's a step that could make the difference between turning up on the first page or nowhere!

Use this opportunity to create a description that echoes the keywords that you've used in your title.

Verify your optimization with Scribe

The tactics I used for most of my blogging career brought in about 28% of my traffic from search engines. At the time I was popping my collar because I thought that was pretty good for someone who really didn't go all out for SEO. I did it when it was convenient or when I thought a particular blog post was important.

Then, out of the blue, I got a client who needed me to write content for his blog. He gave me his bare skeleton ideas and I added the creative pieces that brought it to life. He gave me his keyword phrases that he wanted to rank for and all I had to do was use those phrases several times throughout the post before using this cool plugin that he had installed on his blog.

I'd heard about this "special plugin" but had never had an opportunity to try it out. As mentioned before, I was a bit resistant when it came to SEO, but this client was adamant in using it – he claimed that if it analyzed a post and gave it 100%, he could bank on seeing first page search engine results for his selected phrases. It didn't matter if it was a high competition phrase or not – it was certain to show up and his business depended on it.

First page search engine results? Yeah, right? This, I had to see for myself.

Surely enough, on the day those posts I wrote were published it showed up on the first page for the entire day, many times longer depending on how popular the post was.

I resisted the idea as long as I could – but I couldn't deny it, the plugin worked!

This plugin I'm talking about is Scribe and ever since I started using it over a year ago, I've seen an increase in search engine traffic. About six months after I started using it, my Google Analytics revealed that nearly 43% of my traffic came from search engines! But recently, I've discovered that number has increased to 58%.

I'm sure there are sites that are doing a lot better than this, but this is an improvement that can't be ignored. I'm no longer a skeptic and I no longer hate the optimization process because all of the guess work is gone.

Scribe tells me exactly how to optimize my posts –
Sometimes, I take its advice and sometimes I don't. But by analyzing my posts' content, it's also allowed me to mentally acquire the skills to optimize my posts the first time around – it's

like being back in school – I get that tingle of joy every time I see 100% pop up on the screen the first time.

I'm always late to the party when it comes to new things like this – I always resist until I have proof that a product really does what it says it will.

You probably already know about Scribe and are already reaping the benefits, but perhaps this will help some of those who have been struggling. You don't have to wrack your brain with ineffective methods or accidental overstuffing of your keywords – you can get the perfect balance. If you have the budget to invest in this plugin, it's worth it.

Time to Take Action
Content generation is an Ongoing Task

Now that you've acquired some ways to optimize the content you create, it's time to take action. Gather your team and start generating as much quality optimized content as you can.

Frequent blog updates are essential for building and growing your blog's audience.

During the first few weeks of your blog's existence, it's essential to keep your blog updated. If you choose to post twice a day this week, you can adjust your schedule next week (or the following week, if you're up to the challenge) and post only once every weekday.

If you choose to post once a day during this week, you should continue posting once every weekday until then end of the 10-week challenge. Then you can reduce your frequency to one you intend to sustain long-term (i.e. Three days a week, twice or once a week).

This will give your blog the boost it needs. During this time of frequent postings, you should notice your Alexa ranking improving every day. If you continue completing the tasks each week, you should continue to see improvement with each passing week.

By the end of the Week 2 Challenge during the contest, the leading blog had an Alexa ranking of 429,524! This blog's ranking improved from a number that was in the millions to this six digit figure in just the first two weeks of its existence – now that's results!

Week 2 Challenge Recap:
Quality Content Generation
- Publish 1-2 posts per day
- Optimize your posts for search engines

Week 3 Challenge: Social Proof

Take a closer look at any successful blog. Click a few blog posts, look around and I'll tell you what you will find there:

- Active Twitter counters, usually in the triple digits
- Lots of Twitter followers
- Lots of Facebook Likes/Fans
- Lots of RSS subscribers
- Lots of comments (unless they've disabled them)
- Lots of people interacting with each other

A successful blog doesn't have to boast about how successful it is. It already has evidence: social proof. These days search engines are paying more and more attention to social proof. A blog that can produce evidence that people are enthusiastically sharing its content and lots of it – is a blog that will flourish.

So this week's challenge will require you to further explore those social networking sites and get people engaged and interacting with your content.

Your goals this week:

- Publish 1-2 posts per day.
- Get new Twitter followers.
- Get new Facebook fans.
- Get new people to Google+ circles.
- Get more retweets.
- Get more FB Likes.
- Get more Google +1s.
- Get more comments on your blog.

- Apply this concept to all social networks that you've joined.

Working to develop "Social Proof" is another essential ongoing task.

You should continue to increase your following and content sharing on social networks.

In addition to the above tasks, you should still concentrate on producing 5-10 new blog posts this week.

So you're probably wondering, how to get more followers, fans, retweets, likes, etc.

Here are some social networking sites that can help you get started:

EasyRetweet

Getting retweets is not as difficult as you may think it is. If you produce quality content, people are naturally going to want to share it. The only problem with a new blog is that because the audience is still small, getting enough people to share your content is the biggest problem. The good news is that you don't have to wait for search engines to send you traffic – you can go and bring in your own referral traffic, by using various social networking sites.

EasyRetweet.com is a social networking site that you can join and see results the same day. It's a retweet exchange site that has some great features to get you well on your way to getting more exposure to your blog and fast.

In just a matter of days, I gained over 100 new Twitter followers and so many retweets of my messages, that I lost count. I've also found some new and interesting people to follow and I'm looking forward to continued use of the site.

The site uses a credit system that members use to motivate others to follow and retweet content. You can earn enough credits to get retweets, or you can even purchase a credit package if you're trying to save time.

As you gain or purchase more credits, you use those credits to:

- Gain more followers.
- Promote your best blog posts.
- Promote your ebook or other product.
- Promote a contest entry.

I'm sure you could add to this list. Using the EasyRetweet site is super easy, simply follow these steps to create your account and start retweeting:

1. Visit EasyRetweet.com and sign in with your Twitter account.

2. Edit your profile.

3. Claim 50 free credits or complete additional tasks to get more!

4. Browse Retweets to earn more credits – choose to either "RT Now" or "RT Later." Earn even more credits by following, retweeting, and recommending others. You also earn credits every time you refer a new member to

EasyRetweet. Check your affiliate link, under "My Settings" to obtain your referral link.

5. Add your own tweets and start getting retweeted!

6. Earn or buy more Credits and repeat this process again and again!

Another useful site for getting more retweets:

JustRetweet

Justretweet.com is another retweet exchange site that's very similar to EasyRetweet. It has a similar platform, so I won't walk you through this one and the principles are the same - you can either earn or buy credits there also. I recommend joining both sites for double the exposure.

- For timeless tips for getting more retweets, read:
  "10 Tips to Getting More Retweets"
  http://www.twitip.com/10-tips-to-getting-more-retweets/

- For tips on how to get people to click your links on Twitter, read:
  "7 Tips for Tweeting Links that Get Clicked"
  http://www.trafficgenerationcafe.com/tweeting-links-get-clicked/

How to Get the Most Out of Social Media:

Many people think using social media is all about them and promoting their businesses, their blogs, or whatever else. They tend to view social networking sites as free advertising outlets.

They tend to blast people with annoying messages that do nothing except get them UNFOLLOWED!

Understanding the "social" aspect of *social media* will help you develop beneficial relationships that can help you take your blog's community to new heights.

Why is it so important to be "social" and develop relationships with other people?

If you want to build a successful blog, you're going to need to build and nurture relationships with like-minded people who will read and share your content.

The #1 secret to building those relationships: HELP
This four-letter word really contains the essential components to building relationships online.

Letter "H" stands for "Helping" others.   Answer their questions, respond to emails and comments. Offer tips for improvement – don't be afraid to share your secrets to success with others. Offer to write a guest post for their blog or invite them to guest post on yours.

Letter "E" - Engage them on your blog and on other social networks. Get to know them by responding to their tweets. Show them that you care by greeting them and thanking them whenever they share your content. If you find something you know they might be interested in, be sure pass it along to them.

Letter "L" - Link to their posts. When creating a related post, it's always nice when you can use another blogger's post as an example or for further reading. You can also write a "link love" post or add them to your blog roll.

Letter "P" - Promote their posts. Retweet and Stumble them (Stumbleupon), share them on Facebook and whatever other social networks you belong to. Invite them to join a group where they can share and promote their best work.

These are not the only things you can do to help other bloggers, the options are truly endless. You'll find that the more you help others, the more they will come to your rescue when you're in need of more social proof.

Apply these tips to every social network site that you've joined and you'll be amazed by the results.

The opportunities that can come from helping others are endless. Give it a try!

How to Get More Comments on Your Blog

When you first start blogging, you tend to assume that every visitor who stumbles upon your blog will leave beautiful, complimentary comments on your blog. Then, once you've published your first post you quickly discover that even if people are reading your content, it doesn't mean they comment.

It can be frustrating to not get any feedback. It can make you believe no one cares about what you're writing – but don't take it that far and don't take it that personally. There are some simple things that you can do to increase the likelihood that people will leave comments.

Here are some strategies to get you started:

1. End with a question

The first and simplest thing you can do is end all of your blog posts with a question and then ask people to kindly respond in your comments section. You'd be surprised how many bloggers neglect to do this. This lets people know that you want to hear from them. For some, it helps them think of something intelligent to say.

2. Comment on other blogs

The more you comment and interact with other bloggers on other blogs, the more likely those people will get curious about you and will visit your blog. Try leaving comments on 10-20 blogs a day (or set your timer and comment on as many blogs as you can in one hour) and you'll notice a quick improvement.

3. Motivate people to comment

People need to be motivated to do things. If you give people a reason to comment, they'll usually respond. Try ending one of your posts with a cliff-hanger and offer to reveal the answer only in the comments section. Ask them to guess the answer or the ending and then reveal the answers the next day as replies to their comments.

4. Offer Incentives

Nothing works better than an incentive. Organize a give-away and select a winner randomly only from those who have left comments. Obviously, you'll need something cool to give away and you can't do something like this every day, but it's a great way to boost interaction on a new blog.

Try securing a few sponsors who will offer free merchandise or gift cards for your readers. Don't be afraid to contact local small business owners. You'll have a source of free goodies to give away on your blog in no time.

Note: Incentives can be used to increase Twitter followers, FB likes, retweets, etc. Use Rafflecopter.com – it's a free site that makes organizing giveaways super easy. It's also easy to customize and add to your blog. Try it out this week if you've got time.

During the contest, by the end of this week's challenge, the winning team had achieved an Alexa ranking of 269,026 – all as result of following the very same tasks that you've been given thus far. As you can see, a top 100K ranking isn't as far off as you may have thought!

For more ways to use social media to increase social proof for this week's challenge, check out these posts:

- "5 Ways to Increase Your Following on Twitter" http://weblogbetter.com/2012/07/03/5-ways-to-increase-your-following-on-twitter/
- "5 Ways to Use Pinterest to Drive Traffic to your Blog" http://weblogbetter.com/2012/06/15/5-ways-to-use-pinterest-to-drive-traffic-to-your-blog/#comment-39282
- "5 Tips to Getting More Likes on your Fanpage" http://weblogbetter.com/2012/01/05/getting-more-likes-on-your-facebook-page/
- "How I Got 40,000 Fans to My Facebook Page" http://weblogbetter.com/2012/04/16/how-i-got-40000-fans-to-my-facebook-page/
- "Guidelines for Setting up a Facebook Promotion" http://weblogbetter.com/2012/03/30/guidelines-for-setting-up-a-facebook-promotion/

A Word of Caution:
It's super easy to get caught up in the world of social networking – so set your goals for the day and stick to them or you could end up clicking the whole day away without actually accomplishing anything.

It's a good idea to produce your posts for the week before jumping in to social networking. Do this first!

When you do log in to social networks, make use of timers and keep track of your goals – you want to increase your social proof and build mutually beneficial relationships. Set a time limit for each site and spend time doing only those things that will help you reach your goals.

To help you consider ways to balance your time and social networking efforts, read: "Social Media Can Kill Your Blog" http://weblogbetter.com/2010/07/01/social-media-can-kill-your-blog/

Week 3 Challenge Recap: Social Proof

- Publish 1-2 posts per day.
- Get new Twitter followers.
- Get new Facebook fans.
- Add new people to Google+ circles .
- Get more retweets.
- Get more FB Likes.
- Get more Google +1s.
- Get more Comments on your blog.
- Apply this concept to all social networks that you've joined.

Week 4 Challenge: Blog Engage

Blog Engage.com continues to be one of my favorite social networking and voting sites in the blogosphere. It's a really great place to network with bloggers that you wouldn't otherwise have had the opportunity to meet. It helps new bloggers gain exposure even among more established bloggers.

It's a wonderful social networking site that not only gives bloggers an easy way to increase engagement on their own blogs (by including a voting button), but it also can become a great source of traffic if your posts get published.

So, during the contest, I thought this would be a great way for the team to get the word out about their blog and meet some new bloggers.

The teams produced their blog posts as usual, and every day their posts were submitted to the Blog Engage site. Their posts were submitted automatically via the RSS service, so they didn't have to do it manually. They then visited the site and voted on their own post as well as the posts of other members. Most of their posts received enough votes to be published – securing even more exposure and also a link back to their site – adding even more benefits.

So here are your tasks for the week:

- Publish 1-2 or more posts per day. The more posts you produce, the more opportunities for earning Blog Engage votes.
- Get as many Blog Engage votes on each post as possible.

- Add as many new friends on Blog Engage as possible. Be sure to follow them on Twitter and other networks if the information is provided in their profiles.
- Continue promoting each of your blog posts using last week's "Social Proof Challenge" tasks. See "Week 3 Challenge Recap."

How to get votes on Blog Engage

It's really easy to get votes on Blog Engage if your content is interesting and has a catchy title. But due to the fact that the site is updating constantly, in order to secure more votes, you need to "engage" and interact with others. To help you out, I've provided a few tips to get you started.

5 Tips for getting more Blog Engage Votes:
- Post a reminder to vote at the top or bottom of blog posts, and encourage blog readers to vote.
- Vote on other Blog Engage posts. The more you vote on other posts on BE, the more likely those people will pay you back with a vote.
- Comment directly to posts on BE.
- Send a private message to different BE members asking for a vote in exchange for voting on their posts.
- Send out tweets asking for BE votes.

Note: Blog Engage is now a paid site.

It requires a small one-time fee to become a member and then has additional RSS services that may interest you. If you don't already have a membership and aren't ready to make this worthy investment, you might consider skipping this challenge and returning to it at a later time. Repeat last week's challenge to compensate.

Week 4 Challenge Recap: Blog Engage

- Publish 1-2 or more posts per day.
- Get as many Blog Engage votes on each post as possible.
- Add as many new friends on Blog Engage as possible. Be sure to follow them on Twitter and other networks if the information is provided in their profiles.
- Continue promoting each of your blog posts using last week's "Social Proof Challenge" tasks. See "Week 3 Challenge Recap."

Week 5 Challenge: Newsletter Subscribers

This week marks the half-way point to the end of your 10-week challenge. Hopefully, as a result of successfully completing your challenges, you've been seeing some great improvements your blog's community, traffic and ultimately, your blog's ranking.

All of your hard work has been geared towards building a solid foundation for your blog and getting it off to a good start.

This week, you'll continue working towards expanding your audience by building an email list.

Building an email list is probably one of the slowest and most difficult tasks when it comes to blogging. It's difficult to get people to give up their email addresses when there are so many blogs already asking for them.

But having an email list that you can contact when you've got valuable information to share or when you need help is essential in maintaining a successful blog. So this week, that's the mail goal – building an email list.

Growing an email list can be frustrating, but don't get discouraged. Rather than focusing on the negative aspects of the task, choose instead to focus only on increase. It doesn't matter if only one person responds to your first attempts at securing new subscribers – that is one more subscriber than you had before and is an accomplishment that is worth celebrating.

So don't get upset if people aren't rushing to sign up, as you continue to gradually build your audience, your list will also grow.

Here's what you need to do this week:

- Sign up for a free account at Mailchimp.com if you don't already have one.
- Continue publishing 1-2 posts per day.
- Locate your list subscribe link and promote your link in blog posts. (You'll need to go to "Lists" and create a new list and/or sign up forms.) Add your subscriber link to the top and/or bottom of each of post.
- Add a sign up form to your sidebar.
- Get as many newsletter subscribers as possible.
- Continue promoting your blog posts using the "Social Proof Challenge" tasks.
- Continue promoting and networking on Blog Engage if applicable.

How to get more subscribers:

- Post a reminder to subscribe at the top or bottom of your blog posts, ask people to subscribe if they enjoyed the post.
- Create a free report to give away in exchange for subscription – this works well. I've created a video tutorial for using Mailchimp to automatically deliver a report or ebook – visit the link below to access it

  http://youtu.be/f9G5-3T3Pno

- Send out tweets asking for subscribers.
- Conduct a giveaway or contest – this will bring the best results.

How to conduct a giveaway using RaffleCopter

Rafflecopter.com has really made organizing a giveaway so much easier. It lets you tailor the entry process so that your blog truly benefits from it.

You get to decide which Twitter or Facebook accounts you want entrants to "like" or "follow".

You can require them to retweet the post, leave a comment or even subscribe to your newsletter list (the goal of this week's challenge).

Offer your potential winner(s) PayPal funds, a gift card, or another irresistible prize and watch the entries pour in.
You can specify how long you want the give-away to run and then, it allows you to randomly choose winners from among the entries and makes it easy to email them.

Visit the Rafflecopter FAQ page to get more details on how to use Rafflecopter.

After this week's challenge during the Surviving the Blog contest, the winning blog had acquired an Alexa ranking of 174,893 and had registered a Google Page Rank for the first time

– starting off with a Page Rank of 2. All of this in just five short weeks!

Week 5 Challenge Recap: Newsletter Subscribers

- Sign up for a free account at Mailchimp.com if you don't already have one.
- Continue publishing 1-2 posts per day.
- Locate your list subscribe link and promote your link in blog posts.
- Add a sign up form to your sidebar.
- Get as many newsletter subscribers as possible.
- Continue promoting your blog posts using the "Social Proof Challenge" tasks.
- Continue promoting and networking on Blog Engage if applicable.

Week 6 Challenge:
Guest Posting, Links and Forums

We're into week 6 and by now, you've probably noticed that each week's challenge builds on previous challenges. But regardless of the challenge, there are essential ongoing tasks such as publishing new posts and promoting those posts via social media that continue to enhance and enrich your blog.

By now you should be seeing more comments and social shares. If at this point, you're not seeing the kind of improvement that you'd like, or if your Alexa ranking is nowhere near what the contestants from the Surviving the Blog contest achieved during the last challenge, it may be time for you to stop and revisit the challenges from previous weeks or increase your posting frequency.

If you're noticing a lag in your team's involvement, now would be a good time to reach out to some new bloggers and see if you can get some new people on board with you. By now, through interacting with other bloggers and your blog's readers, you should have a decent bank of people to contact.

If you're in for the long haul, and are ready to press forward, this week's challenge is definitely going to bring you results.
This week's challenge asks you to do a combination of things. This week, you'll write some guest posts, build some links (you'll do this by adding some links to your guest post), and also visit some forums.

Here's what you'll be doing this week:

- Publish at least 1 post per day.
- Write as many guest posts as you can and submit them to blogs.
- Get as many links to your blog posts as possible.
- Get as much referral traffic from Forums (and other sources) without getting banned.
- Continue promoting your blog posts using the "Social Proof Challenge" tasks.
- Continue promoting and networking on Blog Engage if applicable.
- Continue building your email list.

Guest posting

Hands down, guest posting has had the greatest impact on my blogging. It's helped me build my audience and traffic, network with bloggers I otherwise would've missed, and also brought me some interesting opportunities. As a result of a guest post I wrote on one blog, I was invited to guest post on another with even more traffic. The day that post went live, I received record numbers of traffic.

Through guest posting, I've also been able to build links to my blog without the hassle that comes with a link exchange. Having my name and blog appear on authority blogs such as Problogger.net really strengthened my influence. On the days that my posts went live on that blog, I received an increase in Twitter followers, subscribers and discovered that people began to link to my site on their own.

I think guest posting works best when you do it often – having your name and your blog's name appear in lots of places creates the sense that you are "everywhere" all at once. The more people see your name, the more they begin to pay attention to what you have to say. Eventually, you won't have to guest post as often to create the same effects. I don't guest post as much as I used to, but whenever I do, it always gives my blog a nice boost.

Write Companion Posts

Guest posts should be your very best work. And while you may be tempted to save those stellar posts for your own blog, I encourage you to resist the urge to hoard it. The post will have a greater impact when published on an established blog that you consider to be an authority in your niche. To get the most out of your guest post, so that it leads people to click over to your blog, I suggest writing what I call "Companion Posts" – a pair or series of related posts – one to be published as a guest post, the other(s) to be published on your own blog.

For the guest post, write a "teaser" article – one that highlights the benefits of a particular strategy or method. It should build up the reader's interest so that by the end of the post, they'll want to know how to do it – that's when you lead them to the post on your blog where you actually walk them through it step-by-step or provide another in-depth comprehensive link list. Really any "must-read" content will do, but it must have a catchy title.

Write this "how-to" (or other in-depth information) post for your own blog that shows people exactly how to do it, step by step. Then be sure to include the link to this "how-to" post at the end of the guest post. It'll encourage more people to visit your site. I've done this before and it works every time.

This will be the most important thing you do for your blog, so spend some time carefully thinking about where you'll guest post and what you'll write. Do your best to make it stand out, but at the same time still fits within the topic scope of the blog you've chosen.

When the post gets published, promote it with the same vigor and strategies that you use to promote a post on your own blog.

How to Find Places to Guest Post

Finding the right place to guest post makes a major difference. You don't want to spend your time writing your best post for a blog that gets less traffic than your own blog. You also don't want to write a post for a blog that has nothing to do with the topic you're writing about. You want to find a blog that has a good mix of interactivity and a good flow of traffic.

There's no way for you to know exactly how much traffic a blog gets without having a look at the stats for yourself. If this information isn't provided for you, it would be rude to ask the owner, but you can get an idea of how much traffic a blog receives by checking its Alexa ranking at Alexa.com. Just type in the blog's URL and check it out.

Since every bloggers niche isn't the same, there's no way for me to be able to give you the names of the best blogs for you, but I can give you a list of sites to start with.

Submit a post to MyBlogGuest

MyBlogGuest.com is a very unique site that helps bloggers in two ways:

- it's a site where bloggers can offer guest posts to other bloggers (useful when you don't know where to guest post).
- it's a site where bloggers can find guest posts to publish on their own blogs (useful when you need more content for your blog).

The site is free to join and is a great place to network.

Check IblogZone's List

Francisco Perez created a short list of sites that are offering guest posting opportunities in the blogging niche.

http://www.iblogzone.com/2011/06/best-sites-guest-posting-opportunities.html

Check this List of 100 Blogs

Anil Agarwal created a list of various types of blogs that are accepting guest posts.

http://bloggerspassion.com/list-of-100-plus-blogs-that-allows-guest-blogging/

The list includes the blog's Google Page Rank and the Alexa ranking – so he's done a good deal of the work for you. You just need to visit the blogs he's listed and contact the owners.

Guest Posting Tips and a Script

1. Decide on a few places that you'd be interested in writing a post for. They must be places that you already read regularly and have already been participating in the community by commenting, tweeting, or otherwise engaging with the owner and other readers.

So don't submit any "drive-by" guest posts to blogs that you don't know much about simply to get some quick referral traffic. Take the time to develop some relationships and get a feel for the type of posts that are appropriate there.

2. Do a little research on the blog. Look through the archives of the blog to see if there are already tons of posts on your idea. If so, see if there is some angle that has been ignored and then make that the focus of your post. If you choose to write the post, be sure to demonstrate that you are aware that the topic has been previously discussed, but point out why your post is different. This will help your post stand out.

Research will also help you tailor the guest post to the blog so that it's apparent that you are a part of the community and are aware of the overarching theme of the blog.

For example:
When I wrote a guest post for FuelYourBlogging.com, I had a great idea to use the blog's theme in my title and throughout the post – I wrote, "5 Ways to Refuel Your Blogging," (http://www.fuelyourblogging.com/5-ways-to-refuel-your-blogging-efforts/) after taking a moment to look through the archives to make sure no one else had already written a post with a similar title. I was very excited when I found that no one else

had – so it made the post that much stronger because I was able to integrate the blog's theme in a unique post.

Optional: You may opt to contact the blog's owner prior to writing the post to see if they are indeed interested in reading a post from you. This is not necessary in every case – especially if there have been recent posts calling for guest posts or if there is a prominent link to "Guest Posting Guidelines" somewhere on the blog. You'll need to feel this one out – sometimes I contact the owner before I write and sometimes I don't.

Whenever I submit a post without a prior email, I often include a very quick note. I think it's a bit cold to just drop off a guest post with no introductory information whatsoever. My note will usually go something like this:

Good morning (afternoon/evening) BlogOwnerName,
I've truly been enjoying your blog, I've been a subscriber for howeverlong and I really enjoy posts about XYZ. If you're still accepting guest posts, I wrote a post that I think might be a good fit in the XYZ (or ABC) category and I've attached it to this email.

Please review it at your convenience and let me know if you'd like to publish the post. Regardless of what you choose, I'll still be a loyal subscriber, so there's absolutely no pressure. Just let me know what you'd like to do one way the other.

Have a great day!
Kiesha - weblogbetter .com
(You may tweak this note to fit your purposes and use it if you'd like.)

3. If you are going to write the post before contacting the owner and have tailored to post specifically for that blog, keep track of those passages so that you can easily go back and tweak it for another blog if they reject it.

4. Write the guest post and make it your best work. Don't just slap anything together and call it a post. Use humor where possible and add your personality to the post. If you can make an intelligent use of an unexpected analogy, do so. You want readers to be drawn to you. If you do this successfully, they'll follow you on Twitter and become subscribers of your blog – these are indicators of a successful guest post.

5. Include an "About the Author" blurb that has the following elements: Your name, a sentence or two about who you are and what you do, a link to your blog, a link to your blog's feed, and your Twitter username. Keep in mind, however, that some sites will only allow a certain amount of links or may not allow any at all, but include it anyway with a note that the owner may omit it at their discretion (unless, of course, they've specifically stated that they won't accept links).

6. Don't take rejection personally, (don't expect rejection either) that's why it's important to have a few blogs you'd like to write guest posts for so that you can simply move on to the next blog (after tweaking of course, see step 3).

Optional: If you will be submitting to an A-list or other high traffic blog, you might want to give a time limit for a response. For example, you could include a note with your submission, letting them know that they have a week (or even two) to let you know one way or another whether or not they'll be posting it. Let them know that after that time, you withdraw your post. That way, if a month passes with no word from them, you can consider it automatically withdrawn and then you are free to submit it elsewhere or use it for you own blog.

Whatever you do, don't annoy the blog owner with constant emails asking about the status. Either sit tight and be patient, or withdraw your submission.

As you can see, guest posting is a process that takes more than the time to write and submit an email to the blog owner. It actually requires you to know a little bit about the blog you're writing for. But don't shy away from it – guest posting has brought me more positive results than any social networking site or SEO combined. If it wasn't for a single guest post that I wrote for FuelYourBlogging, you probably wouldn't be reading this and I wouldn't be writing this ebook. If you don't know the story of how a guest post turned into an offer to take over WeBlogBetter, read about here:

"Introducing Kiesha"
http://weblogbetter.com/2010/02/17/introducing-kiesha/ .

By the way, I love publishing guest posts, so if you're interested and you've got great insights about blogging or social media you'd like to offer, submit them by visiting the Submit a Guest Post (http://weblogbetter.com/contribute/) link on my blog.

For more tips, visit this link for more blog posts about guest posting: http://weblogbetter.com/topic/guest-posting/

Link Building

When it comes to link building, it's always better when people just naturally link to your content without you having to ask them. This may sound impossible, but if you're producing quality, informative content with catchy titles and you're promoting those posts so that they are seen around the web, then this will happen more easily and faster than you think it can.

That's why it's important to continue the ongoing "Social Proof" promotional activities presented to you during the third week. If you've been doing those things and simultaneously producing quality content, you've probably already secured some links and may or may not even know it. WordPress makes it easy for you to see incoming links, so if you haven't already checked that section of your Admin Dashboard, give it a check. You'll most likely find this information if you've installed the statistics portion of WordPress's Jetpack plugin. Periodically, you may get a "Pingback" email from WordPress when someone links to your content.

If you've got the time to inquire and want to see if there are other bloggers interested in exchanging links, I'd encourage you to do that – but in my opinion, it's not the best use of time. I like to do things that have multiple benefits so guest posting is best choice. You're guaranteed to score at least one link to your blog when you include it in the body of your post or in an About the Author section. So spend most of your time this week working on writing some awesome guest posts.

Tips for getting traffic from Forums

Joining a forum is a great way to meet new bloggers and generate some referral traffic to your blog. But you can't just dive in and start tossing your links around. You've got to engage with others and offer valuable information – otherwise you run the risk of quickly getting banned.

In some forums, your access may be limited until you reach a certain number of posts. You may not be able to start new threads, but you can reply and post in existing threads.

Before you start posting, take the time to complete your profile, just like in other social networks. Add a photo of yourself and don't forget to add a signature – this is where you can add a brief description and a link to your blog.

When you're ready to start posting, refrain from linking to your blog within forum posts. This may cause you to get banned. The best thing to do in a forum is to read through some of the threads and look for questions that you can answer. Look for people you can connect with. Visit the links in their signatures and check out their blogs. Share their content on social networks and comment on their blogs.

Use the forum as a way to demonstrate your level of expertise in your niche and to meet new people.

Forums to join and try out:
- http://www.websitebabble.com/
- http://www.blogengage.com/forum/index.php
- http://myblogguest.com/forum/index.php

These are just a few to get you started. Try conducting a search on Google to find more niche specific forums.

By the end of this week, during the Surviving the Blog contest, the winning team achieved an Alexa ranking of 149,894!

Week 6 Challenge Recap: Guest Posts, Links, and Forums

- Publish at least 1 post per day.
- Write as many guest posts as you can and submit them to blogs.
- Get as many links to your blog posts as possible.
- Get referral traffic from Forums.
- Continue promoting your blog posts using the "Social Proof Challenge" tasks.
- Continue promoting and networking on Blog Engage if applicable.
- Continue building your email list.

Week 7 Challenge: Insane Traffic Generation

This week's challenge is simple – generate an insane amount of traffic! How exactly are you going to do that? By reviewing and applying all of the techniques you've learned so far and using them to the fullest capacity.

This week's tasks:

- Publish at least 1 post per day.
- Use every strategy you've learned so far to get as much traffic to your blog as possible.

Tips for getting traffic from various sources:

During the Surviving the Blog contest, I called upon Ana Hoffman of TrafficGenerationCafe.com to bring in some expert traffic generation tips. She produced three amazing videos that provided great strategies for bringing in traffic.

The strategies Ana mentions:

1.   Send Automatic Direct Messages to Your New Followers
When someone new followers her on Twitter, she uses MarketMeSuite.com to automatically send a Direct Message that provides an incentive to visit her blog.

Her new followers receive cool messages such as *"Wow, thanks for the follow. Feel free to promote yourself here on my blog."*

Visit this link to check out the video for more details:

http://youtu.be/1kdRad9DvYA

2. Easy and Effective Blog Commenting

Visit a popular blog with lots of comments. Don't just leave a comment that responds to the author of the post, but instead, try to extend the discussion by replying to some of the other commentators. Answer questions or extend the conversation by adding strategies or tips that the author may have left out.

Visit this link to check out the video for more details:

http://youtu.be/xpNEtg3B7Zs

3. Article Marketing

Write a post about a current event and publish it on an article directly. You'll need to choose a popular article directory that gets lots of traffic and then choose a popular topic or one that is currently trending right now.

Visit this link to check out the video for more details:

http://youtu.be/K9XTEnkbq3E

Here's the link to the post she mentioned in the video:

http://bit.ly/uKAKm5

Getting more traffic to a blog is the number one concern of bloggers everywhere. I've spent many days searching for a magic traffic trick that could shoot my blog virally through the blogosphere – I've learned the hard way, that there's no magical solution. Generating traffic comes from consistent application of the strategies you've been learning throughout this book.

I highly recommend adding Ana's strategies to the ones we've been exploring in earlier weeks. Use them to get as many people to your blog as possible this week.

For more information on traffic building, I recommend visiting Ana's blog at TrafficGenerationCafe.com or browsing posts in the Blog Traffic Category (http://weblogbetter.com/cat/blog-traffic/) at WeBlogBetter.

Week 7 Challenge Recap: Insane Traffic Generation

- Publish at least 1 post per day.
- Use every strategy you've learned so far to get as much traffic to your blog as possible.

Week 8 Challenge: Networking Blast

Last year, I wrote a post called 7" Signs You're a Hacker & 5 Ways to Use it to Your Advantage" as part of a cross-blog series with bloggers: Hector Cuevas, Ana Hoffman, and Alex Whalley. It turned out to be such a successful series, that I thought it would be great if I could get an A-list blogger to check it out and share it. I gave it a try and was able to get Darren Rowse of Problogger.net to tweet the post to his followers. The traffic boost and the exhilaration I felt that day: unmatchable!

And that is the inspiration for this week's challenge:

Your goal this week is to get noticed by a celebrity or an authority blogger (A-list blogger) in your niche and then get them to share your content. For most people, this is more of a challenge to really get out of your comfort zone when it comes to networking and interacting with bloggers or people you consider a celebrity or another authority figure.

Let's define a *celebrity* as any famous person that a large number of the population can agree is well-known and has had some coverage in mainstream media.

Let's define an authority or *A-list blogger* as any blogger who owns a blog within the top 5,000 Alexa ranking.

Let's define *sharing content* as either tweeting, liking on FB, +1ing on Google+, or linking to any of your blog posts.

Tasks for the week:

- Publish at least 1 blog post per day.
- Network and connect with some celebrities or A-list bloggers.
- See if you can get them to share your content.

How to network with a celebrity/A-list blogger

There really are no special tricks here – you should approach a celebrity or A-list blogger with the same confidence and respect you'd use to approach any other blogger. It works best if you've already been active on their blog (i.e. left comments). Try sending an email that invites them to join the conversation or chime in with their expertise regarding a particular blog post on your blog. If they like the post, ask them to retweet it to their followers. Keep the message short and to the point.

Don't take it personally if you don't get a reply or a retweet, just move on to the next celeb or blogger on your list.

It was interesting to see the way the team members approached this challenge during the contest. They each successfully persuaded some influential bloggers to share their content and by the end of the week, the blog ranked 108,408!

So plot out which celebs/A-list bloggers you're going to contact this week and put this plan into action.

Week 8 Challenge Recap: Networking Blast

- Publish at least 1 blog post per day.
- Network and connect with some celebrities or A-list bloggers.
- See if you can get them to share your content.

Week 9: Promotion on Steroids

This week's challenge will be a combination of everything we've done so far. This would resemble the periodic super-promotion you'd do if you had an ebook or other product you wanted to promote. It's also good to do when your blog has reached a ranking plateau and you need to push through to the next level.

Tasks for the week:

- Publish at least 1 blog post per day.
- Open your blog to guest posters.
- Get as many page views as possible.
- Get as many comments as possible.
- Get as many shares as possible (Tweets, FB Likes/Shares, +1s, LinkedIn shares, etc.).
- Get as many Blog Engage votes as possible (if applicable).
- Get as many links as possible.
- Get as many new subscribers as possible.
- Guest post as many times as possible.

How do you manage to do all of this?

Yes, there's definitely a lot on your plate for this week's set of tasks, but if you could achieve an Alexa ranking of 96,121, as the contestants did by the end of this week during the Surviving the Blog contest – would you think it was all worth it? If it meant you'd have a blog that has a stable readership that can now be monetized – would it increase your motivation?

The best way to approach this week's challenge is to divide your tasks and address a different set of tasks on different days this week.

Here's how I suggest spending your time this week:

Saturday/Sunday
- Write or schedule this week's posts.
- Write 2-3 guest posts to submit to popular blogs.

Monday
- Submit guest posts.
- Create a "Guest Post Guidelines" page and announce that your blog is now open to guest posters. (for more details see "How to Create a Guest Posting Guidelines Page" p.88.)
- Spend a couple of hours promoting via social networks.
- Spend some time networking on Blog Engage.

Tuesday
- Set a timer for 60 minutes to comment on as many blogs as you can.
- Visit EasyRetweet and JustRetweet and post some messages for others to retweet.

Wednesday
- Browse and post some threads on your favorite forums.
- Set a timer for 60 minutes to spend promoting via social networks.

Thursday
- Visit some new blogs in your niche and connect with 10-15 new bloggers/commentators.

Friday
- Complete miscellaneous tasks (blog maintenance, responding to comments, reviewing guest posts, etc.)

Why Open Your Blog to Guest Posts?

Even if you have a great team of bloggers who are consistently submitting blog posts, it's still a good idea to open your blog to guest posters because there's no such thing as too much content.

As I mentioned at the beginning of this book, the more frequently you can update your blog with quality optimized content, the more organic traffic you'll receive. It also gives your readers more to choose from and more to share. If you can get to the point where you're publishing 3-4 posts a day, it won't take you long to see boosts in traffic and advertising potential.

And if your team runs out on you, you'll always have fresh content to post no matter what. Opening to guest posters is a great way to build your blog without having to work so hard.

Of course, opening your blog to guest posters shouldn't just mean free content. You should be creating mutually beneficial relationships with the people who want to contribute to your site. Allow them to include up to 3 links to their site in either the post body or in their bio. Then promote the post as diligently as you would if you'd written it yourself so that they can benefit from the exposure on your blog.

You'll get to keep your site updated and they'll get to borrow your audience for a day.

How to Find Guest Posters

Announce it!

Start by creating a Guest Posting Guidelines Page and add a highly visible text link or clickable graphic to your homepage. Then announce it on your blog by writing an "Open to Guest Posts" blog post that links to the guidelines page.

Tweet and announce it on social networks. Include an announcement in the first newsletter you'll be challenged to send out next week.

MyBlogGuest

Remember Week 6's challenge when I introduced you to MyBlogGuest? I mentioned that it was a great site that helped bloggers in two ways – by giving them a place to submit a guest post and also providing a place to find guest posts to publish on their own blogs.

I use MyBlogGuest periodically when I want to present a fresh voice on my blog. I've also entered and won the $1000 grand prize in a guest hosting contest that simply required me to publish a guest post that I'd found on the site and promote it the same as I would any other post. I won a great prize and I didn't even have to produce the content myself. Who could pass up such a deal?

So whenever you're in need of a guest post – even if no one has submitted one to your blog, you can visit MyBlogGuest and secure a few. It's quick and it's free.

Get Your Blog Added to a List

During the same challenge, I gave you links to two blogs that had created lists for guest bloggers. My blog is listed in both of those. One blogger chose to list my blog on his own, but the other I had to contact myself and ask to be added to his extensive list. Both of those links, as well as a few others, appear in my referral stats quite often and I'm sure has brought in new guest posts for my site.

Here are those links again:

http://www.iblogzone.com/2011/06/best-sites-guest-posting-opportunities.html

http://bloggerspassion.com/list-of-100-plus-blogs-that-allows-guest-blogging/

Try contacting the owners and ask them to add your blog to the list if it fits within the niches they have listed. Then conduct a search for sites that accept guest posts in your niche and see if you can get your blog added to their lists.

How to Create a Guest Posting Guidelines Page

To avoid a lot of confusion and time wasted rejecting irrelevant guest posts, it's a good idea to create a page that specifically explains the guidelines and procedures you'd like people to follow when it comes to submitting a guest post to your blog.

You may be reluctant to put a lot of time and thought into this page, however, if you've been completing all of the challenges and following the strategies, you're on your way (if not already) to having a popular blog that people will want to contribute to. It may start out slow, but before you know it, you could get bombarded with guest post submissions.

Without an organized approach for handing them, you could frustrate or alienate your readers and potential contributors, unnecessarily.

Many new bloggers would tell you that they'd love to have the problem of too many guest posters, but the reality is that it takes time to process those submissions. You've got to set aside time to review, edit, if needed, and schedule those posts. Then you've got to notify the guest to let them know when the post will go live and remind them to stop by the reply to comments. Add these tasks to your already overwhelmed schedule and you've got a recipe for disaster.

Nothing feels as discouraging as having a contributor withdraw a blog post because it took you too long to respond. And nothing is more irritating than discovering duplicate content.

I've had both of these things happen to me and took them as signs that I needed to get more organized.

So I revamped my requirements for submission along with the method of submission.

Here are my suggestions for what you should require from every guest author before you agree to review a post:

Guest Post Submission Requirements

These are the basic things you should ask for on your Guest Posting Guidelines page:

- **A photo or a logo** to accompany their bio – I prefer a photo of a real person, but I realize some people wish to remain anonymous, so a logo is acceptable. I refuse to even look at a post written by someone or somebot who doesn't have either.
- **At least a 2-3 sentence bio.** If they can't tell me about themselves, I begin to wonder why exactly they are so interested in guest posting on my blog. My readers want to get to know and connect with the guests, only spambots would miss this opportunity.
- **They must agree to potential edits.** I care about what my visitors read and if I can eliminate unnecessary errors, then I'm going to make changes. Sometimes I overhaul whole sentences, paragraphs and add links where I deem appropriate. Anyone who wants to guest post on my blog needs to be okay with that.
- **Post must be relevant to my blog.** I don't have time to read posts about where to get the best credit card deals because it has nothing to do with my blog. It doesn't matter how good the post is, I can't use it! People (or spammers) who haven't noticed that WeBlogBetter is about blogging and related topics obviously haven't really read my blog, so I'm not really going to read their post – or respond to their inquiry for that matter!

These are the things I require, but you should take some time to think about your needs. You could start with what I have, but feel free to add to it.

Guest Post Submission Methods

You have various options to use for your submission method and procedures, but you should consider the pros and cons of each to determine which will work best for you.

Submission Form:

When I first began accepting guest posts, I used a submission form similar to a contact form. It automatically emailed the guest post text and info to me. I would review the post and then if approved, I would upload the post and notify the author of the publish date.

It worked for a while, but quickly got out of hand when guest post submissions increased.

Pros:
- It was simple to set up
- I didn't have to grant the author access to my blog.

Cons:
- Uploading posts became very time consuming.
- Sometimes the posts got lost in my overflowing inbox.
- Required me to upload author bios and photos.
- Lots of spam submissions.

Contributor Registration:

This is the method I use now, but I had to make quite a few tweaks before it began to run smoothly. When I first opened my blog to registrants, I'd set it to automatically grant contributor access, before I knew it, I had tons of spam and irrelevant submissions!

Now, I only allow people to register as subscribers and then they must request access. This decreased spam submissions, but doesn't come without drawbacks.

Also, for those of you who are unaware of user roles in WordPress, it's best not to grant access above "Contributor" – this grants the least amount of access needed to submit a post.

Pros:

- Contributors can upload their own posts, so this saves time.
- WordPress automatically pulls in photos from Gravatar.com or the guest's WordPress profile.
- Contributors can enter their own bios.
- I can use a plugin to automatically email contributors when their posts go live.
- Contributors are emailed when comments come in, so they're more likely to respond – saving me additional time.

Cons:

- Time needed to upgrade registration from subscriber to contributor.
- I periodically have to clean out spam subscriber registrants.

Feel free take a look at my guest post submission instructions – copy and tweak as needed: http://weblogbetter.com/contribute

If you follow these strategies you'll have more guest posts than you can use in no time.

Week 9 Challenge Recap: Promotion on Steroids

- Publish at least 1 blog post per day.
- Open your blog to guest posts.
- Get as many page views as possible.
- Get as many comments as possible.
- Get as many shares as possible (Tweets, FB Likes/Shares, +1s, LinkedIn shares, etc.).
- Get as many Blog Engage votes as possible (if applicable).
- Get as many links as possible.
- Get as many new subscribers as possible.
- Guest post as many times as possible.

Week 10 Bonus Challenge:
Newsletters & Monetization

During the Surviving the Blog contest, Week 9 was the final challenge, but I've added this week's challenge to help you build a solid foundation for monetization.

Most bloggers hope to build a successful blog that generates income. And while there are tons of get rich quick schemes that surround this industry, I know from experience that it's not that easy to get rich quick and be both legal and ethical.

I like the idea of being able to sleep at night, guilt-free, so there will be no turn-key to overnight riches hype here. But the strategies I offer will help you begin to create opportunities and generate income that will increase over time.

This week, you'll focus on various strategies for earning an income and will also touch bases with your newly acquired subscribers.

Here's what you'll need to do this week:

- Publish at least 1 post per day.
- Send out your first newsletter to commemorate your completion of this book's 10-week challenge. Write about your experience and highlight 3-5 of your most popular or recent blog posts.
- Brainstorm on how you will use your skills and talents to generate an income.
- Set up various monetization accounts (Google Adsense, PayPal, Sponsored Reviews, etc.)
- Continue promoting your blog posts using the "Social Proof Challenge" tasks.
- Continue promoting and networking on Blog Engage if applicable.

- Continue building your email list.

Get in Touch with your Subscribers

Hopefully by now you've got at least a few new names in your email list. It really doesn't matter if you have 2 or 20000, now is a good time to connect with those subscribers and let them know that you intend to stay in touch.

How Often?

If this is your first time emailing your subscribers, this is a good time to let them know what to expect. Decide on how often you will email your subscribers and stick to it. Some say once a week is good, while others think once a month is less intrusive. I tend to only email my subscribers when there is something noteworthy to tell them, but I don't think that's the best frequency. The point is, find what works for you and commit to that.

What information should go in a newsletter?

There really isn't a set format for sending out a newsletter. But there is some basic information that you should probably include in each one.

A Catchy Subject Line

If you expect your email to get opened, you're going to have to make the subject line very eye catching. Most people get tons of emails every day - most of which they consider junk, so if you don't want your newsletter to get ignored, you'll have to make it sound irresistible.

Don't over-do it, or you could run the risk of sounding like spam. Avoid words or phrases such as "free" or "get paid" or you'll run the risk of triggering the spam filter – your email will never get read, then! Use your own email opening habits as a rule of thumb, if it sounds like one you'd like to open, go with it.

What's Useful/helpful

People may have signed up to your email list because they were hoping to get ideas or tips from you. Don't disappoint them – every now and then, treat them to some content that you've created just for them. Keep it short, but helpful.

What's New?

Let the word "news" guide you – so talk about what's new at your blog. What new projects are you working on? Any new series in the works? Are you participating in any contests that you need help promoting?

Recent Posts

Include teasers to your recent or most popular posts if your goal is to get them over to your blog. Don't assume that your subscribers have been visiting – this is a good way to get them back.

The above items are the bare minimum. Customize and add your own ideas. The goal is to keep it interesting to make sure your emails stand out in a crowded inbox.

Why did they Unsubscribe?

There are hundreds of reasons why a person might unsubscribe to your email list. They may have forgotten that they subscribed in the first place. They might be in a bad mood. They might be trying to clean up their inbox. Or they simply no longer need the information. No matter what the reason, try not to take it personally.

I know… it still stings when I see people leaving my list, but sometimes, it's just unavoidable. I consider it a necessary part of developing a responsive list of subscribers who actually open and respond to your emails. What good is a subscriber who doesn't want to open your emails, anyway? I'd rather that they unsubscribe to make room for someone else who really wants to hear what I have to say.

I suggest changing your list settings so that you only receive a notification when someone subscribes – not when they unsubscribe.

Tips for Generating an Income

A while ago, a guy contacted me asking me how he could earn money from his blog. He needed some answers. He asked:

Is it really true that you can make money blogging and if so, how much can a person expect to make and how long would it take?

I had to be honest with him. While yes, you can earn money from your blog, it certainly doesn't happen overnight, a week or even months for some people. There was no way I could give him an accurate prediction, and even though it was an opportunity to gain a new paying client, I refused to candy coat the situation.

Regardless of what others might do to earn money, I refuse to steer someone wrong solely to make money. There are internet marketing blogs that make honest money, but I don't condone any purchasing programs that promise quick and easy money – because now that I know what really goes into blogging, I know that for the average person, those programs are bound to fail.

How do I know? Because I've been there and done that – spent it and lost it and I refuse to be the cause of someone else doing the same.

Instead, I told that gentleman that if the focus of the blog was on producing quality content, information, or products or services that provided solutions, then yes, it is possible to earn money from your blog. But earning the money can't be the sole focus – people can sense when someone is just out to get their money. Helping people and providing useful information should be the focus, instead.

That's why I chose to leave monetization for the end of this book. Any attempts to monetize before your blog has a solid foundation will only alienate people who might've been interested if only they'd had to time to build their trust in you.

After you've earned enough trust amongst your readers, at that point you could begin monetizing your blog with ads, affiliate links of reputable products and also by creating quality products such as e-books, and by offering your services.

Offering your services to your audience has the greatest potential for generating income. If you're good at what you do, even if you offer free tutorials for completing a task, some people would rather just to pay you to do it for them. That's because everybody can't do what you do and do it well.

I've learned that lots of people hate writing, so I have offered my writing services to them so that they can continue to publish fresh content on their sites. For the people who don't mind writing, but need someone to go behind them and polish it for them, I offered editing and proofreading services. Then there are the people who want a blog, but don't have a clue how to get started, I help them by installing and designing their blogs for them.

So how can you take what you already know how to do well and start earning money from your blog?

Here's some tips:

1. Create a "Hire Me" page for your blog that outlines and explains the type of services you provide. Based on your experience and level of expertise in the field of your choice you could offer services that range from freelancing, writing, editing/proofreading, consulting, photography, anything really… that logically relates to your blogging niche.

2. Include a contact form that let's potential clients contact you for a quote. Or you may include prices on this page – however, if you'd prefer to negotiate prices on an individualized basis, I suggest omitting figures.

3. Make sure a link to the "Hire Me" page is visible within the top fold of your blog for easy viewing.

4. Promote your services by writing a blog post that presents the benefits of your services. Will your services save time? Make life easier for your clients? How will your services compare to what others are doing?

Be sure to tweet and share this post on all social networks that you're active on.

5. Promote your services further with a giveaway. Give away samples or provide services for free to one or more winners in exchange for permission to include them in your portfolio, list of satisfied customers or testimonials. This is a great way to get great recommendations if you're just getting started.

If you don't like organizing giveaways or contests, you could also sponsor a contest on another blog with your services.

6. Contact a few of your blogger friends and have them write a review of your services on their blog or include you in a list of recommended services or products.

7. Start locally, network among your friends or contact a few people in your area who could benefit from your services. Hand out some business cards and offer discount services in exchange for referrals. If you do a good job, word will spread fast.

These are just a few tips. If you're creative, there are no limits to what you can do to create your own job opportunities and earn more from your blog.

Take some time to brainstorm and answer this question:
What services could you start offering today?

Various Ways to Make Money with your Blog

In the beginning, when most bloggers first install WordPress, they are filled with a sense of excitement and hope. They rarely envision themselves a year, two years, or even three years later, still struggling to make money blogging.

Even if the goal isn't to be the next guru making a six-figure income, most bloggers at least hope to make a little extra spending money.

As each day that rolls by without any affiliate sales or ad revenue, causes bloggers become frustrated and begin to question why they ever started blogging in the first place.

Yes, they certainly wanted to share their knowledge and unique perspective with the world, but also possibly, to get a little more exposure; to grasp some new opportunities or maybe even a book deal.

After the initial excitement wears off, it becomes harder to find the motivation. That's when a blogger meets the crossroad: to quit or keep blogging?

Those who keep blogging are the ones who love it with or without pay – but wouldn't it be great if they could get paid?
If your blog isn't making money, it could be because you are putting all of your efforts into the wrong income sources instead of building multiple sources.

When I ask bloggers who approach me with this problem, what they are doing to generate an income, their first response is almost always: *Google Adsense* and sometimes *affiliate links*.

Very rarely are they building their email list or offering valuable and helpful content. They are not offering any services and they haven't made any connections or built relationships with other bloggers in their niche.

Connect and Reveal yourself
It's very difficult to generate an income that way – you can't expect people to jump on your recommendations if you haven't established a connection with them. It's very hard for them to trust you if they still don't even really know who you are – if you

very rarely show your face or express your own opinion on your own blog.

How do you connect and reveal yourself?

This may mean that you might have to lose the logo and trade it in for a fresh photo of your smiling face. Somehow you've got to let the world know that you are a real human.

Get out and visit some other blogs in your niche and leave some comments – make it a point to start getting to know other people.

Don't Just Recommend give the Inside Scoop

I still find it surprising that some bloggers still believe that the banner ads in their sidebar will do all of the affiliate link promoting they need – *wrong!*

Hardly anyone ever really pays attention to those flashing banners over there in the sidebar or even the ones at the bottom of posts. They honestly would rather stick a few hot coals in their underwear than sit there and click one of your ads.
So that means you're going to have to do some work.

Write some posts about those products you want to generate an income from – and not just a "hey buy this new whatchmagigger!" – but actually dig in and give the insider scoop.

Show people what it is that *you* (yes, you!) like about a particular product or service. Describe your experience in vivid detail. That means you're going to have to reveal a little bit about yourself and it also means that you should have some experience with the product or service. In other words, you didn't just join the affiliate program; you actually had an opportunity to try it out before sharing your findings on your blog.

Don't try to say it all in one post

When you're recommending things, it's probably best to do a series of posts. Write one post about one aspect or benefit. Most of us just want to say it all and get it out in one post, but really, it's far more beneficial to do it in pieces. It gives you more than one opportunity to talk about the product and it also signals the search engines that you've got some valuable information that they can send people to check out.

Treat your blog like a business

If you expect to make money from your blog on a steady basis, you can hang up treating it like a hobby, you're going to have to get serious about it and treat it like you would treat any other business.

Create a schedule for yourself that you will stick to and then set some business goals. You can't just expect things to just happen, you've got to strategize and then take action.

Register a business name and track your earnings and expenses so that you are prepared at tax time. If you choose not to register a business name, you'll still need to claim your earnings as "Self-Employment" income.

Diversify your income sources

I don't know about you, but I'd rather make money blogging in steady small portions that add up, than to have one large portion come sporadically. Who cares if you made a $5000 commission one day if that's all you made the entire year? I'd much rather have $20,000 that trickled in slowly from numerous sources.

Take some time to consider your skills, gifts and talents in order to really uncover your income sources.

Here are a few sources that you might want to consider:

Freelance – Offer what you love to do as a service
The bulk of my income has come from the services I offered.

If you've been hoping to generate passive income, then that source will not be a good fit for you. Offering services takes time and energy. But if you choose those services from the activities you already enjoy, you'll be far more successful because you'll finally begin to get paid to do what you love and what you're good at.

Offer a service that will save time or solve a problem and before you know it, you'll have to turn people away.

Write an eBook already!
What if the reason people aren't buying all of those ebooks you're advertising is because they'd much rather read your book? It doesn't have to be New York Times Best-Seller quality, just give it your best professional effort and put it out there. Set up an account at e-Junkie.com and create an affiliate program so other bloggers can help you promote it.

You may not get rich off of this, but at least you'll have one more money making opportunity than what you had before.

Mobile Apps
I hear that developing iPhone and other smartphone apps that relate to your niche is an awesome way to create an income stream that could grow into a flood. You don't have to be an expert, just find someone who is and let them help you. You can

outsource inexpensively by going to Elance.com, Fiverr.com or PeoplePerHour.com.

Plugins
There are some plugins that a blog just can't do without, why not create the next must-have plugin and charge for it?

Enter contests
To some people this might not technically sound like blog income, but if you need a blog to participate, I consider it blog income. There are some pretty big contests going on right now that even if you win the lowest prize, you'll still take home a cool $100 or more.

4 Basic Accounts to Monetize Your Blog
To get you started with your monetization process, you'll need at least these basic accounts. Obviously, any additional accounts should be based on your niche and the products or services you want to promote.

- Google Adsense – Let's you earn by the click.
- PayPal – Let's you collect your earnings. Take advantage of the MasterCard Debit card to have access to your money anywhere.
- PeoplePerHour – Join this site and bid on various freelance opportunities.
- Sponsored Reviews – Join this site and set your price for writing sponsored reviews.

You might also want to check these out to see if they are a good fit for you:

- AffiliateLights - Get $10 just for signing up!

- ClickBank – Find electronic products to promote.
- Linkshare – Various products and services.
- ShareaSale – Various products and services that include Thesis and Scribe.

Week 10 Bonus Challenge Recap: Newsletters & Monetization

- Publish at least 1 post per day.
- Send out your first newsletter.
- Brainstorm on how you will use your skills and talents to generate an income.
- Set up various monetization accounts.
- Continue promoting your blog posts using the "Social Proof Challenge" tasks.
- Continue promoting and networking on Blog Engage if applicable.
- Continue building your email list.

I have good news and bad news…

The good news is that by now, you should have a rapidly growing blog that is bringing in increasing levels of traffic every day.

The bad news is that even though we've reached the end of this book, it is not the end of your hard work. This is not the time to put your blog on autopilot and forget about it.

Hopefully, if you've given each challenge full effort, you should have a blog that doesn't require as much attention as it did in the beginning, but this is not the time to schedule some posts and then leave your blog to fend for itself.

You'll discover that as you continue to blog and continue to network and connect with others that you don't have to work as hard to promote your blog, but you'll still need to spend time attending to some aspect of your blog on a daily basis.

Alexa rankings are not solidified once you achieve them. They can reverse. If you stop updating your blog, as your traffic drops, you'll notice changes in your ranking. The same can happen if you stop promoting your posts – you might be updating frequently, but if enough people aren't visiting your blog, this will also cause your Alexa ranking to deteriorate.

If at this point you're exhausted and need a break, I suggest reducing your time spent on social networks. Schedule two weeks' worth of posts ahead of time and take it easy until you catch your breath.

If you notice your rank deteriorating, organize a RaffleCopter giveaway with self-promotional entry requirements and revisit the "Promotion on Steroids" challenge. This should keep your blog growing and moving in the right direction.

Send Me Your Results!

I've worked hard to bring you the best strategies that I know will work and I'd love to hear about your success!

If you've followed all of the strategies and they've worked for you, contact me and tell me where your ranking was at the beginning and how it improved (Alexa and Google Page Rank).

I'll post your results and a link to your blog on WeBlogBetter.com.

Contact me: kiesha@WeBlogBetter.com

Join the Affiliate Program

Now that you've completed the challenges and know how well they work to build a blog, why not promote the book and earn a 50% commission?

It's easy to join, just visit this link and sign up via e-junkie:

https://www.e-junkie.com/affiliates/?cl=106317&ev=9a0843fdcb

Links mentioned throughout this book:

- Twitterfeed.com
- Naming the Blog
  http://weblogbetter.com/2012/02/10/naming-the-blog/
- A Killer Domain Name: The Most Important Blog Decision
- http://weblogbetter.com/2010/12/13/a-killer-domain-name-the-most-important-blogging-decision/
- Justhost.com
- Netfirms.com
- Genesis Framework
  http://www.shareasale.com/r.cfm?b=386922&u=417520&m=28169&urllink=&afftrack=
- TheNextGoal.com
- Tapestry Theme
  http://www.shareasale.com/r.cfm?b=289123&u=417520&m=28169&urllink=&afftrack=
- Maxblogpress site
  http://www.maxblogpress.com/plugins/mpo/
- Scribe http://weblogbetter.com/go/scribe
- Using WordPress Can Ban Your Blog From Ping Services http://www.maxblogpress.com/plugins/mpo/
- How to Ping Your Blog and When Not To
  http://keepupwiththeweb.com/how-to-ping-your-website-blog-and-when-not-to/
- Top 15 Blog Ping Services
  http://howto.medinfo24.com/best-15-blog-ping-services-to-ping-your-post-immediately/
- FreePrivacyPolicy.com
- The FTC, Affiliate Disclosure & You
  http://blog.2createawebsite.com/2009/12/07/the-ftc-affiliate-disclosure-and-you/
- Twitter.com

- BizChickBlogs.com
- 5 SEO tips for bloggers that won't make people gouge their eyes out http://weblogbetter.com/2010/05/22/blogging-tips-seo-for-blogger/
- Top 10 Free SEO Tips for Beginners (Post Panda and Penguin)   http://www.minterest.com/top-10-free-seo-tips-for-beginners/
- EasyRetweet.com
- Justretweet.com
- 10 Tips to Getting More Retweets http://www.twitip.com/10-tips-to-getting-more-retweets/
- 7 Tips for Tweeting Links that Get Clicked http://www.trafficgenerationcafe.com/tweeting-links-get-clicked/
- Rafflecopter.com
- 5 Ways to Increase Your Following on Twitter http://weblogbetter.com/2012/07/03/5-ways-to-increase-your-following-on-twitter/
- 5 Ways to Use Pinterest to Drive Traffic to your Blog http://weblogbetter.com/2012/06/15/5-ways-to-use-pinterest-to-drive-traffic-to-your-blog/#comment-39282
- 5 Tips to Getting More Likes on your Fanpage http://weblogbetter.com/2012/01/05/getting-more-likes-on-your-facebook-page/
- How I Got 40,000 Fans to My Facebook Page http://weblogbetter.com/2012/04/16/how-i-got-40000-fans-to-my-facebook-page/
- Guidelines for Setting up a Facebook Promotion http://weblogbetter.com/2012/03/30/guidelines-for-setting-up-a-facebook-promotion/
- Social Media Can Kill Your Blog http://weblogbetter.com/2010/07/01/social-media-can-kill-your-blog/

- Blog Engage.com
- Mailchimp.com
- Video: Automatically Deliver Ebook via Mailchimp http://youtu.be/f9G5-3T3Pno
- Alexa.com
- MyBlogGuest.com
- IBlogZone's Guest Posting List http://www.iblogzone.com/2011/06/best-sites-guest-posting-opportunities.html
- List of 100 Blogs http://bloggerspassion.com/list-of-100-plus-blogs-that-allows-guest-blogging/
- 5 Ways to Refuel Your Blogging http://www.fuelyourblogging.com/5-ways-to-refuel-your-blogging-efforts/
- Introducing Kiesha http://weblogbetter.com/2010/02/17/introducing-kiesha/
- Guest Posting Tips Blog Posts http://weblogbetter.com/topic/guest-posting/
- Website Babble Forum http://www.websitebabble.com/
- Blog Engage Forum http://www.blogengage.com/forum/index.php
- MyBlogGuest Forum http://myblogguest.com/forum/index.php
- TrafficGenerationCafe.com
- MarketMeSuite.com
- Video: Web Traffic Strategy 1 http://youtu.be/1kdRad9DvYA
- Video: Web Traffic Strategy 2 http://youtu.be/xpNEtg3B7Zs
- Video: Web Traffic Strategy 3 http://youtu.be/K9XTEnkbq3E
- Post mentioned in Ana's video http://bit.ly/uKAKm5

- Blog Traffic Category http://weblogbetter.com/cat/blog-traffic/
- Problogger.net
- Submit a Guest Post at WeBlogbetter http://weblogbetter.com/contribute
- e-Junkie. om

About the Author

Kiesha R. Easley is the owner of WeBlogBetter.com, a blog devoted to offering blogging, social media, writing, and SEO tips. She blogs there and shares her audience with guest posters.

She is a writer, copy-editor, and a college mass communications instructor. She also advises the student newspaper.

Connect with her on these social networks:
Twitter: @weblogbetter
Facebook: http://facebook.com/weblogbetter
Google: +Kiesha Easley
LinkedIn: http://linkedin.com/in/kieshaeasley
Email: kiesha@weblogbetter.com